# Tropical Fishes As Pets

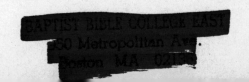

# CHRISTOPHER W. COATES

DIRECTOR

NEW YORK AQUARIUM—NEW YORK ZOOLOGICAL SOCIETY

# TROPICAL FISHES AS PETS

*Photographs by S. C. Dunton*

*Courtesy of New York Aquarium—*
*New York Zoological Society*

**COLLIER BOOKS**
NEW YORK, N.Y.

This Collier Books edition is published
by arrangement with Liveright Publishing Corporation

Collier Books is a division of The Crowell-
Collier Publishing Company

First Collier Books Edition 1962

This book does not purport to be a complete list of the fishes suitable for a domestic aquarium, but is merely a discussion of the possibilities and care of such fishes with a few examples from the various groups.

# Contents

# Tropical Fishes As Pets

# Chapter 1

## Collection of Fishes

### I. Sources

THE COLLECTION of the fishes which inhabit our aquaria is not the least interesting part of the hobby. While very many fishes are bred in commercial establishments, the largest proportion of the species up to the present are caught wild and transported across the oceans for our delectation.

The proportions, however, are rapidly reversing themselves. There are collectors in almost every tropical country—men who are as much at home in the unmapped jungles of the Amazon or Congo as they are on our city streets (and probably quite as safe and comfortable), intrepid souls who match the orchid-hunters in the extent of their wanderings in search of new and rare fishes to send to their houses of business in America or Europe.

These collectors establish stations at convenient ports where there is a fairly regular steamer service, and have the natives of the country catch what fish they can for them, but since most native peoples do not consider a creature under five or six inches long a fish at all, the burden of the searching is done by the collector himself, who teaches the natives that this little water animal with the red stripe or that little one with the big fin is worth a few pennies or cigarettes or whatever may be the current exchange.

When the collector has sufficient fishes to make a shipment, he packs them into cans, usually about twelve or fifteen inches across and four or five deep. These are well insulated with felt or paper wrapping against fluctuating temperature, and so made as to minimize the motion of the boat. The cans are carried aboard and placed in charge of a competent sailor who will take care of the shipment. When large, regular shipments are made, such as between Germany and New York, and when it is not convenient for the ship's crew to watch them, attendants, or runners, accompany each shipment, watching for dead or dying fish which may pollute the water and cause the loss of the whole canful, which may, in some cases, number a hundred or more. The shipments may be of as few as ten cans or as many as one hundred and are not infrequently two, three or even five hundred cans.

## II. Transportation

To transport fish successfully, a man must have an unusual amount of something, which for want of a better name, we may call "fish sense." All successful aquarists have this to a greater or lesser degree, else they could not keep fish at all, but the man who must keep his fish alive in the cramped, awkward cans and quarters of a ship which tosses and rolls continually, must be more than a mere aquarist. Fish are very poor sailors and are invariably seasick, a condition which usually occasions surprise to the uninitiated. The seasickness is not fatal in itself, but the fact that the fish lives and has its being in the water which is then polluted makes complications. To guard against such contingency, fishes are not usually fed for at least twenty-four hours before shipping, so that their stomachs are empty, and they are not fed during the voyage. But if the ship is making a long passage, the fishes must be fed sometime, and the skill of the runner is then drafted to its limit, for he must choose the right moment to feed, and the exact amount for each fish.

Then, of course, the fishes are crowded considerably and quickly use all the available oxygen in the water. This must be replaced somehow. The agitation of the water by the motion of the ship does this to a certain extent, but not enough to keep the fishes alive, so recourse to air pumps is made. The flow of air through the water of each tank must be regulated exactly to prevent the fishes being bruised by violently churning air and water, and to provide them with sufficient oxygen. The sources of air supply must be looked to also, for if the pump intake is near foul air, it will be conveyed to the water with disastrous results. One collector successfully carried about forty thousand fishes from India to Philadelphia, and lost them all by having some of the gas used in fumigating the ship upon its arrival blown through his cans. This collection represented six months' work, endless miles of travel and many difficulties overcome, so it was no small loss.

Another collector, up the Amazon, was almost eaten alive by piranhas, the famous man-eaters, but three or four inches long. Such are the vicissitudes of collecting that his brother, with him on the occasion, did not think it worth mentioning. Incidentally, an infrequent specimen of this genus finds its way to our tanks, but collectors fight shy of them, for they are so fierce that only one may be carried in each can, unless the passage is so rough that they are too concerned with their own misery to bother one another. One fish to a can, ordinarily, is not profitable, so the piranha is somewhat rare in North America.

A fair number of exotic fishes find their way to North American markets through the intermediary of sailors who wish to turn a dollar or who are interested enough to bring them in gratis. Many sailors develop into excellent carriers, and some of them even rig up their own aquaria aboard and carry fish all over the world. Such men are invaluable to scientific institutions, for they will carry fish otherwise unobtainable to universities and public aquaria whose exchanges and requirements are not large enough to warrant the expense of a special messenger. There are, however, occasional snags. One engineer on a large passenger vessel has been carrying fishes about the world for years, and has even persuaded his confrères to board a few when his own cabin is full to overflowing. He refuses absolutely, albeit nicely and gently, to carry fishes for the hospitals, which use these little animals to further research into human diseases.

In general, sailors do not carry very many fishes, for their losses, until they have made several trips, are large, and unscrupulous native dealers at the source of supply often sell them fishes which have no aquarium value, so that all their time and labor is reduced to naught.

## III. The Competitive Fish Market

In new territory the collector frequently arouses the militant suspicion of the natives, since they are often the first white men to visit obscure villages and backwaters. The appearance they present, with their knee boots for wading and their assortment of cans and nets jangling about, must be terrifying indeed. However, the waters of the tropical world are rapidly revealing their finny secrets. If the present rate of exploration continues, there will not remain a stream or pool unvisited or a species of suitable size untried. Many fishes shipped by the collectors do not meet with favor for the same obscure reasons that govern the popularity, or lack of it, of a play or book. And those fishes which do meet with popular approval are constantly being studied and pampered until the best method of raising them is discovered and made public, thus killing the market for that particular fish as far as the collector is concerned. This drives the collector farther afield in his search for suitable material for our aquaria, with the consequent extra risk of losses in the transfer through rough country in the wild to the security of civilization. Because of this risk, the collector must either increase his prices to make up for the extra time and loss, or else go out of business.

Then again, the governments of some countries of supply, discovering that additional revenue may be obtained from the export of these comparatively overlooked natural resources, are making it increasingly difficult for the collectors to obtain specimens of merit.

As an instance, Brazil, the home of the Scalare, found that the value of a pair of these fish was in the tens of dollars a few years ago, but that a sufficient number had been exported free to form the basis of a considerable breeding business. She is now taking no more risks that she will overlook the financial benefits of such a business by placing an export tax on all fishes which leave her shores. This ranges from ten to fifty cents a fish, a considerable sum when one realizes that the tax is paid on all the fishes shipped, regardless of the number which die aboard ship, and which is estimated by importers to be about fifty percent. The tax, then, on the fishes which survive the trip is from twenty cents to one dollar a fish, and if a collector ships in several hundred fishes, after catching and transporting them to the shipping point, paying the tax and freight, and then finds that they do not meet with popular approval, he is at a considerable financial loss.

Even the most astute collectors and dealers cannot gauge the market correctly all the time, and they are sometimes left with a considerable number of really nice fishes which are quite suitable for domestic aquaria but which, for some unknown reason, no one will purchase. If those fish fanciers who are of an enquiring turn of mind and who can afford to do so would take a few fishes of which they know nothing, and which sometimes are completely unknown to science, they may be able to find out some very interesting things which may not always bring in any financial reward, but which would carry the satisfactory knowledge that they are exploring, in their own way, the mysteries of nature.

## Chapter 2

## Assembling an Aquarium

### I. Styles of Aquaria

THE FIRST requisite for the person who intends to keep fish, whether for study or pleasure, is a place for the fish to live in. This, by the nature of the animals, must be a water-tight jar or box. It may be of any shape or material, provided that the shape will allow a reasonable amount of the water to be in direct contact with the surrounding air, and that the material will not throw off poisonous matter when in contact with water. Since most people like to look at their fishes, and most fishes are imperfectly visible from above, the obvious material for a small aquarium is glass, and since the animals do not do well in round affairs, such as jars or bowls unless they are very large, the best shape is square or rectangular. Tanks of this type may be procured at any pet store in a variety of styles, either of all glass or glass sheets held in place by metal strips at the corners. The fishes treated in this book as a rule live nicely in small tanks of not less than two gallons capacity, which are somewhat wider than their height and longer than their width. Since a tank of this description can generally be purchased for less than it can be made, and is usually substantially built and of the right proportions, we will assume that a standard aquarium has been procured.

### II. Water

The next item is the water.

Cold water from the faucet in most parts of the United States is suitable for fishes; so we place enough water in the tank to reach to within two inches of the top. Then, because we are going to assemble a "balanced aquarium," we procure a quantity of fairly coarse-grained sand, thoroughly washed to remove all foreign bodies and dust, and place a sufficient amount in the tank to make a layer of an average depth of about one inch. The order in which the water and sand is put into the tank is immaterial, of course. The sand should be sloped somewhat higher at the back than at the front. This is so that any débris which may accumulate in the tank will be brought together within reach of a siphon.

## III. Sand

The sand in itself is unnecessary to the well-being of the aquarium and is used merely as an anchorage for the plant life which is necessary if the aquarium is to be properly "balanced."

Sometimes small pots of various shapes are filled with sand in which the plants are rooted. These are quite practical, but do not look so well as a sandy bottom. Sometimes, too, a layer of humus is first put down, and then the sand over it. The idea of this is to feed the plants, but since most aquarium plants derive all the nourishment they require directly from the water, soil is not essential. A further disadvantage is that, if the aquarium must be moved, or the sand disturbed, or fish which dig into the floor of the aquarium are used, the soil will be displaced and will spoil the appearance of the aquarium by floating in the water in fine particles and settling over sand and plants.

## IV. Plants

There are many plants which will live in water, but the few best suited to aquarium life have been fairly well sorted out by now. The others seem to require special treatment best rendered by a botanist; so beyond mention of them, we shall not go further into their peculiarities.

The plant Vallisneria or Tape Grass, as it is commonly called, is an excellent plant for domestic aquaria. It has long, slender, flexible leaves which curve gracefully to the movements of the fish. Several leaves part from the crown of the root and grow about twelve inches high. Some species have leaves two or three feet long, but these are not usually encountered. If the aquarium is healthy and there is food for the plants, small runners will also grow out from their crowns. These do not reach the surface, but curve downward to the sand, sending a new system of roots downward and another cluster of leaves upward. Thus is a new plant formed. This continues until, within a few months, the plants growing from the original may number twenty or more, and may be traced all over the aquarium. The runners all grow from opposite sides of each plant, and seldom more than two are observed. Occasionally, one plant in the series will send up a slender tendril which, when it reaches the water surface, blossoms into a delicate white flower with a golden center. Another plant will start with the same kind of tendril, but one which is only about two or three inches long. The slightly bulbous top breaks off and floats to the surface where it opens into a tiny floating flower and drifts, at the mercy of every small current, until it meets the flower at the end of the tendril. These are, respectively, the flower of male and female plants. When the floating male flower touches the anchored female flower, fertilization takes place, and the anchoring tendril is coiled up in a tight spiral, pulling the remnants at the end of the stalk under water again. This happens only after several generations of plants have grown from the runners, and only when an aquarium is in good condition.

As with all plants, Vallisneria seems to grow better if it is planted in fairly compact bunches. The roots of several plants should be placed about one inch apart in the sand, care being taken that only the roots are covered. The crown—the juncture of leaves and roots—should be just clear. This method of planting fortunately lends itself to the artistic arrangement of the aquarium.

A plant similar in appearance but of a sturdier and more robust quality is Sagittaria. There are several species of this plant—also obtainable under the name of Tape Grass—suitable for aquarium cultivation.

One is of about the same height as Vallisneria, but the leaves are broader, coarser and much stiffer looking. Another is of about the same appearance, but the leaves are only three or four inches long. Another useful plant has leaves of about the same length which are much finer and apparently round in cross-section. This is known as "Hair Grass." All of these propagate by means of runners; all are hardy and prolific. By a judicious planting of any of the Sagittarias and a few plants of

Vallisneria, a very beautiful tank may be arranged. The arrangement of the taller plants in the corners and back of the aquarium, with a few clusters of one or another of the smaller types toward the front, is ideal.

Two plants of widely different appearance, but of similar growth procedure, are good. These are Anacharis, the "Water Pest," which grows so fast under favorable conditions that the aquarium soon becomes completely choked with it, and Cabomda, which does not grow as fast but has lovely foliage.

Anacharis has a round stalk with several leaves originating together at evenly spaced distances along its length. These leaves are about one inch long and one-eighth of an inch across and curve back slightly. When procured from the stores, the stalks are in bunches of about a dozen, wrapped together with lead or string. The stalks may be thrust into the sand, after the lead has been removed, where the plant may grow. Fixing the ends of the stalks in the sand or under a small stone is certainly the neatest arrangement in the aquarium, but the plants will grow much more satisfactorily if they are just thrown in loosely. They float to the surface, but send down very thin stalks which find their way into the sand and serve as anchors. When two or three of these are well established, the stalk from which they came will grow in endless convolutions about the tank, and may be cut into pieces, each of which will repeat the process. When this happens, however, the growing end should be used and the rest relegated to a stock tank or thrown away.

Cabomba also has leaves which grow at intervals along a round stalk. These, however, are fan-shaped and split up into hair-like parts. Cabomba sends its anchoring roots down, but usually does not grow as well as any of the others in the warm water of a tropical fish aquarium. When the stalks of either Anacharis or Cabomba are buried in sand, they are apt to turn brown and become slimy and dead, thereby causing a good deal of débris, even if the plant itself does not die.

## V. Light

All of these plants live well in the subdued light of the average aquarium, but they appreciate a stronger light, such as an hour or two of direct sunshine every day or several hours of artificial light. Under light, photosynthesis is set up, and the plants perform their primary function in the tank, which is to fix the carbon dioxide manufactured by the fish. They also liberate a quantity of oxygen; but this will be treated in another chapter.

When a strong light is not available, or where the artistic layout of the aquarium calls for it, a different plant may be used. This, Cryptocoryne, thrives in shady places, and has broad leaves, each at the end of a separate stalk which grows directly from the crown of the plant. This plant seems to require little light in the performance of its function. The leaves of Cryptocoryne are a dark, lustrous green, and, if it can be made to grow with other plants, it is an effective foil to the lighter, more delicate green shafts of the various Tape Grasses suggested.

This plant should also be planted quite closely, in clusters of several roots, buried, as in Vallisneria. If it establishes itself, it will send out runners in several directions along or just below the surface of the sand. Each of these runners will start another plant into being. A good strong plant with a number of leaves may be divided into several separate plants, each of one or two leaves, by splitting at the roots, or the runners may be cut and the young plants transferred to other aquaria. The runners of all these plants may be cut without injury; thus an aquarium can be thinned out and another stocked with the young plants without loss. All of these plants are rooted, or at least have anchorages. There are a few other useful plants which float and, while not being immediately necessary to the orderly establishment of the aquarium, should be borne in mind for their potential value when young fish are to be reared or a variation in the appearance of the tank is desirable.

## VI. Floating Plants

Probably the prettiest floating plant, with considerable value as a nursery of baby fish, is the Crystalwort, *Riccia fluitans*. This is a tiny plant of slender, branching stems, which probably should be called leaves, since there is no apparent difference between stem and leaf. A cluster of these inch-long plants, an intricate mass of delicate green, is an impenetrable refuge for small fishes which can find their way along the water paths without fear of hungry mouths snapping them up. Under a fairly good light, Crystalwort will spread completely over the surface of an aquarium to a depth of two or three inches, sometimes shutting off the light from the plants below.

*Utricularia minor,* the Lesser Bladderwort, is also an invaluable plant for the aquarist who likes to raise his own fish. This plant does not grow as compactly as does the Crystalwort, and its mass of stalks and foliage are much more graceful and airy. For fishes which spawn on plants, the Lesser Bladderwort is excellent and the interstices are just as safe for tiny fish as are those of the Crystalwort. This Bladderwort has a larger relative which must never be used near small fish, for it has the unpleasant habit of snaring them into the spring-lidded pods and digesting them. However, this meat-eating plant is not widely available, so there is no need to worry about it.

## VII. Miscellaneous Plants

A number of other plants are occasionally available but are of little value, other than esthetic, to the aquarist. These include Salvinia, Azolla and Duckweed, all plants which grow on the surface of the water, also Hornworts, Myriophyllums and Ludwigiæ, which need not be rooted but are submerged, growing like Anacharis and Cabomba.

Why plants are necessary to the aquarium may not be apparent at first glance. It is obvious that they beautify an aquarium, just as they add a note of cheer and freshness to a room, but some of the lifelike glass and porcelain imitations are just as lovely, and have the added advantage of never dying or turning brown. Then, too, many people consider the aquarium incomplete without a miniature ruined castle, bathing girl or Grecian pillar placed at strategic points. These may seem beautiful, but they are useless to the man who wants his tank to be a complete microcosm.

The plants in the aquarium serve the same purpose in the water that leaves do in the air. They fix and break up the poisonous by-products of living animals. Specifically, they use, when photosynthesis is stimulated by light, the carbon-dioxide released by the fishes. They also liberate oxygen. But this is part of the chemistry of water, a sufficiently important subject to the aquarist who wishes to proceed intelligently to warrant a chapter to itself.

# Chapter 3

## The Chemistry of Aquaria

### I. Gases

WHILE AN aquarist may not be, even in the remotest way, interested in chemistry, or may have but a wholesome awe of its difficult names and horrible odors, his aquaria are complete manufactories of the most obscure biochemicals and his fishes active, albeit innocent, workers in these factories. Most of their products, by bulk, if not by number, are quite common, well-understood gases, of which water will carry a more or less constant amount.

We have all watched the tiny beads of air forming inside a glass of iced water left standing too long, and we have seen bubbles rising and bursting in a pan of warming water. These bubbles are dissolved gases being driven off as the temperature increases. Cold water will dissolve more gases than warm, and releases them readily as the temperature increases.

The chief gases which ordinary tap water contains are oxygen and carbon dioxide. The first is in comparatively small proportion compared with air; the second in large proportion.

Aquatic animals are almost all aërobes; that is, they breathe and must have air or the oxygen contained in air. There are a few anaërobes—animals which can live without oxygen—but they are not fishes and therefore not our concern.

As the fish swims, he uses oxygen, which must be replaced. This is done by the surface film, by the process known as osmosis, a Greek word derived from "to push," which means, in simple language, that the gases in the denser medium tend to flow to the thinner. In this case, water, which will not dissolve more than, say, six parts per million of oxygen, is under continual pressure by the surrounding atmosphere to absorb more oxygen. The atmosphere has about two hundred thousand parts per million of oxygen. Then, as the fish use one part of the water's six, a replacing part flows into the water from the air.

As the fish uses the oxygen, it makes carbon dioxide, another gas, which is lethal—not poisonous but suffocating. This, too, is subject to the laws of osmosis. Water under ordinary circumstances dissolves a certain quantity of carbon dioxide—much more than is in the air. We will say that there are twenty parts per million of carbon dioxide, called $CO_2$ by chemists, in water, and only a trace in air. This, then, reverses the oxygen process, and the air is under constant pressure by the water, to take $CO_2$ from it. As the fish makes additional $CO_2$, the pressure on the air increases and we have the $CO_2$ being released from the water. However, oxygen invades water almost instantaneously and much more rapidly than $CO_2$ evades it. Unless, therefore, we have an auxiliary method of releasing the pressure of $CO_2$, the fish will build up a suffocating environment and die.

Plants provide this auxiliary release of $CO_2$ by using part of it as food, but they only do it when they are in a fairly good light, so that we have the major vexatious difficulty of our aquarium's chemistry neatly solved by placing a few stalks of green leaves in it and leaving it where it will get a decent light.

As we have seen, the oxygen in the water is replaced almost immediately it is used by more from the air, so the little that is given off by the plants, or most of it, bubbles to the surface and is gone. It does, however, serve some purpose, for, as it rises, it makes tiny currents in the water which help to bring each particle of water into direct contact with the air and thus assist in the release of the $CO_2$. This interchange of gases between water and air brings us to another horrific chemical problem.

## II. pH

As $CO_2$ is an acid gas, the accumulation of it tends to increase the acid content and decrease the pH, the present stalking horse of the well-informed aquarist. ("p" means potential; "H," hydrogen, and the combined letters have been neatly translated into "the log of the reciprocal of the Hydrogen Ion concentration." It has also been translated into whole books of chemical formulæ so I don't think we'd better do anything about it except to use it as a hook on which to hang the acidity or alkalinity of water.) The subject of pH is complicated, worthy of the most advanced chemist, but its ramifications, in regard to the aquarium, are not as hopeless as they seem. By the same process of osmosis—the forcing of fluids from the denser to the lighter medium—our friend the fish is an integral part of his environment. He lives in it and breathes quantities of it, even, according to some authorities, eating or, rather, drinking part of it. However, since all of the fish exposed to the water is a permeable substance, subject to the laws of osmosis, he must be in exact chemical balance with his surroundings. If the water content, then, is highly acid, and the fish is highly alkaline, the interchange of chemicals—gases, salts or whatever—will be so violent that he will die unless he develops a special armor to protect himself. Very marked differences are not usual, but they occur when a deep-sea fish is placed in fresh water or vice versa. Small changes are quite common. If we take a fish from a slightly acid stream or pool and put him in a neutral or alkaline water, the various pressures which occur may not be sufficiently severe to destroy the animal, but they may inhibit some of his functions. Likewise, if we take a fish from alkaline water and put him into water which is alkaline but which is allowed to build up an acid condition by the accumulation of $CO_2$, we may be putting him under a strain which taxes all his endurance to support, leaving none for the important function of reproducing his kind. This is a theory only. We know about the osmotic pressure, and we know that many fishes will, and do, live for years in an aquarium without breeding, but so far very little work has been done that ties these two facts together.

There are many chemicals which will alter the pH of water. Some of these chemicals, such as caustic lye, will run the pH up quite high, and will also kill the fish. Others, such as hydrofluoric acid, will take it down considerably, with equally tragic results to the fish. However, a few chemicals alter the reading one way or another without very drastic effects on the fish. Some of them change the pH for a while, but are absorbed by the plants as food and so rendered innocuous. Hence, the aquarist may take an interest in the pH of his aquaria without losing a great deal if that interest is purely academic, unless he wants to breed fish as a commercial enterprise, when the approach would necessarily be different from that outlined in this volume.

## III. "Buffers"

Of much more importance to the fish than the pH reading is the amount of "buffer" present in the water. While these are responsible for the pH reading, they do not show up on the ordinary pH scale which runs from 0 to 14.

If we take a sample of water which is entirely free of any acids or alkalies, and make a pH test of it, the reading will be at 7, the neutral point. Now if we add a definite quantity, 1, of acid to the water and read it again in our testing apparatus, we will have a pH reading of 6. If we then add a proportionate amount of alkali to our water, the reading in the apparatus will be at 7 again, just as it was before we added any chemicals at all, although there are now equal parts of an acid and an alkali. Now, if we add to the water two more parts of acid, and only one part of alkali, the reading will show 6, as it did when there was only one part of acid, although there are now three parts of acid and two of alkali. This runs all the way through the pH scale, which is, after all, merely a statement of the excess of free acids or alkalies only and not of the kinds or quantities. The quantities of acids offset by alkalies, or vice versa, are known as "buffers" and are very important for the tank. Fish are not concerned with the excess of either of these things. They are concerned only with the total amounts of each, for, returning to our laws of osmosis, if there is a higher concentration of chemicals in the water than there is in their bodies, the chemicals will be forced into the fish, and may destroy them, while if there is a denser concentration in the fish than in the water, the water will absorb the excess to the discomfort of the fish.

## IV. Osmosis

This osmosis takes place through the various osmotic membranes, which practically cover the animal, but are particularly concentrated about the head—in the gills, for instance, which expose to the water a considerably larger area of skin than is at first apparent.

An example of this chemical change in the water and of the varying ability of different fishes to withstand the differential osmotic pressures, was recently afforded.

An explorer of very distinguished ichthyological attainments found on an island in the West Indies a lake of perfectly fresh water, but with an unusually high concentration of common chemicals, mainly chalk. In this lake were living very many marine fishes. Samples of the water were brought to New York and analyzed, both quantitatively and qualitatively, and a quantity of the same kind of water made (synthesized) from the bottles and jars of the chemist's laboratory. Into this mixture of fresh water and chemicals a few common goldfish were put. They lived in apparent good health. Then to the goldfish were added a few specimens of marine fishes, none of which was represented in the island lake. These also did well, apparently finding nothing in the treated fresh water to upset their salt-water conditioning. Then another sea fish was added to the collection. This also lived well as long as it was undisturbed, but at the slightest nervous shock, such as the clapping of hands three feet away, it turned on its back and died—immediately. The other fishes were unaffected.

Such an effect as this cannot reasonably be accounted for by any ordinary explanation, but if we accept the fact that fishes are in osmotic balance with their environment, and that there was a chemical present in the system—probably the nervous system—of the fish, but not in the water, nor in the other fishes, and that the water took from the fish sufficient of the chemical to balance itself with the fish, the latter, if it was unable to obtain more of such a chemical or chemicals, would be left with a deficiency great enough to cause its death under the slightest strain. Such an explanation would support the theory of "buffers," for the pH values of the manufactured water and the water from which the fish originally came were substantially the same.

## V. Chemical Factors in Breeding

It has been shown many times that fishes live fully and normally in a great variety of waters of all sorts of different pH readings. It has also been shown that certain fishes live in all sorts of waters of different pH readings, but do not live fully; that is, they do not breed, unless the water is of a definite pH, when kept in aquaria. A consideration of the factors involved in the course of a fish's normal life may help us to understand some of the seeming anomalies.

Observers, earnest and competent, have recently found that the Scalare, at once so easy to keep and so difficult to breed, will breed freely if it is kept in an aquarium of slightly acid water. From shape and habits of the fish, as well as the reports of collectors of this species, it is logical to suppose that the fish lives in water which is fairly still. Such water, at least in wooded country, is usually considerably shaded from the sun by surrounding trees, and has, besides, a considerable quantity of fallen leaves floating about on the surface. Still water, in these conditions, would probably build up a considerable concentration of $CO_2$, which in turn, would make the water of a low pH reading, or acid in quality. Because the general tendency of the pH of the average aquarium of decent size is upward, by reason of the heavy growth of plants encouraged which absorb the $CO_2$ under the strong light to which they are usually subjected, and the fact that these fish do not usually breed in aquaria, it was reasoned that the addition of a little chemical of an acid nature could be made with profit. This proved to be the case. When harmless acids such as monosodium phosphate were used in sufficient proportions to bring the readings of the pH comparators to about 6.0 or 6.2, no harm was done, and the fish started to breed. The danger of such procedure is in the assumption that all fish like such water, for a fish from a similar locality to that from which the Scalare comes, but in which there are probably many more dead leaves, has spawned in water which is consistently alkaline in nature. This is the Leaf Fish, *Monocirrhus polyacanthus*, which seems to show a preference for alkaline water, for it eats well and has spawned and the young have hatched in water well above neutral on the scale, while it seems to lose its appetite in water which runs below neutral. The scale readings may mean nothing, or they may mean much, but the difference in the activity of the animal is much more likely to be due to the difference in the "buffers," the total of the ionized acids and alkalies, rather than to the amounts of either in excess.

## VI. Adjusting the pH

Then, of course, not all acidulous chemicals are equally harmless. While it is perfectly safe to use one, it is just as unsafe to use another. This should always be borne in mind when making pH adjustments. The particular chemical mentioned, monosodium phosphate, is usually broken down to its components and utilized by the plants as food, so the addition of small doses from time to time will not lead to the destruction of the life of the aquarium.

It is necessary to explain that if the aquarist is working with pH, it is essential that he take his readings at some regular time of day, for the readings in an aquarium in early morning, before the daylight has started the plants photosynthesizing, will be more acid than they will be at night in the same aquarium because the plants have been using the carbon dioxide built up during the dark hours as food during the hours of strong light.

There is one other chemical which may cause the aquarist a certain amount of trouble. Many cities use chlorine to purify their water system, and occasionally more than is actually necessary is used. This may run through the piping system to the faucet from which the aquarist draws his water, and if it is not eliminated, will cause the death of the fish. A little care is all that is required. If this poison is used in the water supply system, fish should not be placed in water drawn straight from the faucet, even if the temperature has been adjusted. The water should be drawn and splashed about a little and then left to stand for a while, perhaps as long as a week, although this period is usually unnecessary. If a few plants are left in the water, or any organic matter, the free poisonous chlorine will either be released as a gas or will be changed into a usually harmless chloride. We say "usually" advisedly, for it is only when the chlorides are exposed to a few metals, such as zinc, that they become poisonous. In the average aquarium, these metals are not present, the only things exposed to the water are the inert glass and sand and the living plants and fishes.

While this whole chapter on aquatic chemistry may seem extraneous in a book of fishes, or superficial to the biochemist, a few words about what is going on in the aquarium may serve to allay the fears of unchemically minded aquarists who are exposed to conversation about pH and kindred subjects and are scared thereby. After all, many fishes have been born, have lived and reproduced their kind, and have died in aquaria long before there was any talk of the chemistry of water. It is nice for those who are born with a questioning mind to find out the reasons for thus and so, but they can always pursue their investigations through the medium of the technical literature and their own experiments without spoiling the fun of those who keep fishes in their homes solely as a means of diversion.

# Chapter 4

## Fish Diseases and Diets

### I. General Considerations

LIKE ALL other animals, fishes are subject to diseases. These vary considerably in their cause and in their manifestations, and although each may be well understood academically, the prevention and cure of fish diseases is not easy. In general, it is better to throw out a fish that is very sick, rather than try to treat it and run the risk of infecting all the fishes in the aquarium. However, some of the diseases react favorably to fairly easily applied treatments, and many people never like to admit that they are licked, so for their guidance and not as a treatise on fish diseases, we shall include a few words on the more general ills and their treatments.

It should be remembered at the outset that nothing is a sure cure for any specific disease. With all our elaborate, splendidly equipped hospitals, and the attention and skill of the finest and most painstaking medical men, we cannot always discover the origin of, prevention or cure of a common cold.

As with human ills, prevention is easier than cure, so if we will only keep our aquaria in fairly decent condition, and see that none of the fishes is bruised or chilled, we have done about as much as we can to keep the fish in good health. The rest—treatments of one sort or other—help, of course, but there can be no guarantee of success with the most highly recommended of them.

### II. Treatment by Drugs

Because of the close relationship between fishes and their environment, from which they are utterly unable to escape, treatments by drugs and chemicals should be approached with extreme caution. For instance, ordinary Epsom salts are frequently used for fishes, the doses being often given at regular intervals. Since the fish is part of its environment, and the salts, going into solution, become part of that environment, it will be evident at once that some of these salts will always be present in the water after they have once been added, for even when the fish swallows the whole quantity of the drug, part at least is passed back into the water to be re-swallowed by the fish every time he opens his mouth—fairly frequent phenomena, as you know. Thus the fish will be under continual treatment whether he wants it or not.

Of course, if the fish is treated in a special aquarium, and replaced in its own after treatment, such a reabsorption would not take place, but the strains and stresses on the physiology of the fish in the change from one tank to another are sufficient, very often, to be the cause of numberless weaknesses, in themselves harmless, but rendering the fish open to attack from other bacteria or parasites which are always in the water of an aquarium. These weaknesses are, of course, most apparent in the species of fishes which are comparatively rare, and for this reason most subject to attention; so the net gain of any treatment is problematic in the extreme.

Still, everyone likes to do all he can for his pets; so we shall outline a few general hints.

## III. Apparatus for Treatment

Every aquarist in the least interested in the well-being of his fish should have one or two shallow trays or dishes in which to render the proposed aid. The reason they should be shallow is that in this type of container there is a larger surface area in proportion to the body of water, and this will mitigate against the evil results of small bodies of water by decreasing the amount of suffocating carbon dioxide in the water. This is a primary condition for the good health of the fish.

## IV. Fish Medicines

The amount and numbers of various fish medicines necessary is entirely up to the aquarist, who, if he can distinguish between the various spots and marks of different kinds of parasites which infest sick fish, will be that much nearer to a cure, for almost every disease germ has its specific poison. The trouble lies in the fact that so many different diseases have the same general appearances that it is impossible, without the aid of a well-equipped bacteriological laboratory, to distinguish one from another. Then we have to resort to a general germicide of sufficient virulency to kill the disease without damaging the fish. These are not easily measured; so there is not much to do, unless the disease can be definitely identified, but use a relatively harmless chemical like common salt, which is an excellent tonic for sick fish, and of considerable germicidal power as far as fresh-water bacteria are concerned. This will not work if the fishes are too sick; but in this case, the probabilities are that nothing will, for the necessary handling on top of the sickness is pretty drastic for a weak animal.

However, we take our sick fishes and place them in water as nearly similar as possible to the water from which they came, and add sea salt if any is available. This is because there are other salts of value in the sea besides the sodium chloride of commerce. Lacking sea salt, we may use rock salt in preference to table salt, for this latter has often a modicum of other chemicals in it to keep it from caking or to iodize it. These additional chemicals may be harmless, but we do not require them. Whatever salt we use, the quantities are approximately the same. About one teaspoonful to a gallon of water is sufficient for minor attacks, and a tablespoonful to a gallon of water is permissible, if the condition of the fish warrants it, but this quantity is rather heroic and should only be tried in extremity. The salt may be added to the water of the aquarium, but since it never goes away again, unless the tank is taken down completely, it is more advisable to administer the treatment in a special tank. One of the trays, for instance, may be used for this purpose. After the fish has recovered and the water has been thrown away, the fish may be returned to its fresh-water aquarium.

The salt treatment is used for a number of parasitic distresses as well as fungus, and if the hospital tank can be heated a few degrees, the effects are considerably hastened. The heating should be done carefully, and not to a point where the fish is in apparent distress. In any case, an increase of fifteen degrees Fahrenheit is usually high enough. The high temperature should be held for four or five days, and then gradually lowered to normal. (All the changes should be gradual, or the fish will become ill from the sudden change alone.)

## V. Fungoid Diseases

The indication of fungus is the presence of a white scummy substance growing over the fins. As the progress of the disease increases, the body is attacked, and then the fish is usually in a bad way. The fungus is fairly easily removed by the salt in the early stages, but with much more difficulty when it has taken hold of the body proper. This disease is very contagious, spreading through a tank of fish with alarming rapidity. As the fish are observed to be attacked, they should be removed for treatment, and the whole tank treated with a little salt. If the sickness is not noticed until some of the fishes have died, all the fishes had better be treated, and the tank taken down and thoroughly disinfected with strong salt or peroxide solutions or a coarse soap.

## VI. Parasites

"Ich" is frequently spoken of in connection with aquarium fishes, but its presence is not as frequent as might be supposed. The symptoms are tiny white spots scattered over the body of the fish, but while this Ichthyophthirius is indicated by these small white spots, not all white spots indicate Ichthyophthirius. However, these are all usually caused by protozoan parasites which imbed themselves in or just under the skin of the fish, and most of them will react to the salt treatment outlined previously.

These particular parasites have been found to react strongly to a short exposure to aqua-flavine and some of the citrates, but the use of such potent drugs in the hands of the inexpert almost invariably leads to trouble, so they better be left alone; the simpler treatments usually meet all the needs of the average aquarist.

Parasites, the presence of which may often be observed without the use of a glass, are harder to remove, for they can, under unfavorable conditions, cover themselves with an impervious membrane which resists almost all attempts to remove them. They may be removed by mechanical means, either by being picked off or by rubbing the fish down the scales, as vigorously as the fish can stand, with a bit of cotton soaked in a disinfectant.

Another method of removal of parasites and bacteria is by changing the water in which the fishes live at regular intervals of several hours. This is effective against those causes of disease which have a free-swimming period in their lives. As they are born and are passing through this stage, they are washed away, and the old ones, already firmly attached to the fish, live out their lives and die without being replaced by younger ones.

## VII. "Green Water"

The "green water" which occurs at least once in the life of each aquarist is not to be despised as a tonic for sick fishes. A fish which is not exactly ill, but which is not in very good health, will respond quickly to a holiday of a week or two in a tank in which the water is so thick that the fish cannot be seen. Of course, such a tank is unsightly in the extreme, but if one can be stored away where it gets a strong light, and is not subject to much temperature difference, it will be found very suitable for a hospital tank. If there is any sediment at the bottom over which a catfish is continually working, the effect will be that much better, for fishes generally do not live in quite such clean water as we endeavor to supply them with in our aquaria. The presence of the catfish will limit the possibility of the tank fouling for these fishes eat every bit of organic matter they find, leaving none to spoil.

## VIII. Prevention

However, prevention of sickness is much more effective than attempts to cure it; so if the aquarium is kept at a fairly constant temperature, and the fishes fed upon suitable food, varied occasionally, and a scavenger fish or two is kept in the aquarium to eat up all the wastes, the likelihood of any disease obtaining a strong hold in the aquarium is considerably lessened. If there are a number of aquaria in use, the utensils which may be moved from one to another should be kept soaking in a disinfecting solution when they are not in use, so that any parasite that might take hold in one tank will not be carried to others by the nets or thermometers which are often dipped from one tank into another.

A small container full of water to which a few drops of mercurochrome, permanganate of potash, or even a little common salt has been added is all that is necessary to wash the nets in.

## IX. Food

The question of feeding tropical fishes calls for some little consideration by the enthusiast who intends to keep fishes of many different kinds. Not all fishes will eat the same foods. Fortunately, however, most of the popular fishes will eat a great variety of easily procured foods, and those fishes that will not are usually acquired only by the expert who has some experience of the different diets required by fishes.

For the most part, our pet fishes will thrive on the types of food put up in small containers and retailed at small cost. These are combinations of meats, cereals, eggs and fish, in different proportions, and are very easily handled. When a diet of these dried foods is offered the fishes, it is wise to vary the brand somewhat, for the different ingredients and methods of preparation are usually such as to destroy some of the qualities requisite for the good health of the pets. This lack is inherent in the foods themselves, for no matter how good and wholesome the original material of which they were composed, such foods are, after all, thoroughly dried and lack the elements of living matter which are so important to the health of the fish.

Still, most of the smaller fishes of the aquarium will live and rear offspring if they are fed on these dried preparations almost exclusively. But if they are so fed, it is always a good plan to give them an occasional meal of living matter in the form of Daphnia, Tubifex or Enchytræn worms, or ordinary garden worms, raw lean beef, clams, oysters or shrimp chopped up fine. The former group is available in most pet shops and may be used as purchased. At all times it is axiomatic that if a supply of live food is available, it should be used in preference to any prepared food.

When regular foodstuffs are used, they should be chopped on a board with a sharp knife, for most meat grinders will not produce fine enough bits and some of the fishes may choke in trying to swallow them.

If Daphnia is procured, and there is more than the fishes can eat, it may be stored in cold water through which a stream of air is flowing or even in the fish tank itself, for any of these minute crustaceans that are not eaten will live in a well-kept aquarium indefinitely, and the fishes will pick them up when they get hungry.

Tubifex worms may be stored in running cold water, but more than the fishes will eat should not be placed in the tank at one time. These will live in water, but they require more dirt than is ordinarily left in the aquarium, and if they dig under the surface of the sand and there starve, they will make the tank malodorous.

Enchytræns will live in moist humus, and may be reared in sufficient quantities to feed a number of fishes in a small wooden box. This should be partly filled with good black earth, slightly dampened, and the worms fed with a little boiled oatmeal, bread soaked in milk, thick, sour milk, or foodstuffs of a similar nature. Care, however, should be taken that the soil does not become sour or closely packed. These worms will not live more than one day or so in water, so more than the fishes will eat at one time should not be placed in the aquarium.

Very small fishes, such as the fry of the egg-laying species, require small particles of food. Some of the finely-ground prepared foods are suitable, but in any good healthy aquarium that is not less than a month old there is a great quantity of minute organisms on which the fishes will feed. In fact, enough of these are constantly being produced in such an aquarium to keep a fair-sized brood well supplied with food until the individual fishes composing it are big enough to eat the smaller particles of the food supplied to their parents. Where there is not sufficient, the lack may be made up by using infusoria. This is easily produced in a small container. A small quantity of hay or a fresh lettuce leaf should be placed in a jar and some warm water poured over it. The jar should then be left to stand for a few days, after which a number of small, whitish creatures may be observed swimming about in the water. Then a small quantity of the water should be poured into the aquarium and the fry will immediately devour all the animalcules developed in the jar. This feeding should be done in small quantities several times a day or there is danger that the water in the aquarium will be spoiled.

Such comparatively large babies as those of the livebearing fishes will eat worms almost immediately after they are born, so there is no problem involved in their feeding.

However, it is much more important to know what not to do than what to do. Most fishes will adapt themselves to almost any kind of food and, unless they are actually poisoned, will live surprisingly long on most unsuitable diets. They will not live in foul water, however, and the most usual cause of foul water is the addition of larger amounts of food than the fishes can consume. This uneaten food becomes the focal point for all sorts of bacterial populations which soon spoil the water for the fishes and cause their untimely demise.

If fishes are acquired about which one knows nothing, it is essential that some idea of what they eat be acquired at the same time, for appearances are often deceptive and it does not always follow that a fish which looks ferocious is as bad as he looks. An instance was afforded by some Gobioides which were brought into New York by a sailor. These were taken from a native collector who had no idea from whence they came. They had not been fed on the boat. Their long, speedy shape suggested that they caught living fishes, or at least insects, for their food, a supposition which was born out by the large, cruel-looking mouth from which a series of teeth protruded. However, a number of guppy introduced into their tank remained uneaten, as did a number of large aquatic insects. After close observation, it was discovered that the fishes used their large mouths as a sort of plow with which to scour the bottom of the tank and scoop up débris of all sorts, upon which they seemed to thrive.

In contrast, the innocent-looking Leaf Fish refuse to eat anything but the most lively of smaller fishes, not even bothering with a fish which is not actively swimming about.

Always ask the person from whom the fishes are procured what they have been eating, then, after you have them firmly established in your aquarium, experiment with their diet if you must.

# Chapter 5

## Viviparous Fishes

### I. Community Fishes

FOR MOST people, to whom space is a consideration and who, after once having become addicted to the collection and breeding of tropical fish, are not content with one or two kinds of fish, the community tank, with its collection of varicolored and differentiated fishes, is the best answer to the problem of keeping as many fishes in as little space as possibe.

Many fishes included under the general title "Tropicals" are of a peaceful nature—at least as far as fish of a comparable size are concerned—and will live in perfect harmony with other fish of their own or of different species, while many are so ferocious that they will attack their own shadows if reflected in a mirror. Such animals as the latter are, obviously, unsuited to community life, and if they are kept at all, must have aquaria to themselves, just as other anti-social animals are segregated. However, since most families of fishes have at least one or two amiable representatives, a collection of the most diversified, interesting and exotic specimens from all the warm fresh-waters of the world may be built up and maintained in one aquarium.

A tank holding fifteen or twenty gallons of water is ideal for such a collection, and if a little judgment is exercised as to the type of the specimens selected, the tank will present an ever-changing lesson in natural history, as colorful and spectacular as a "Follies" show.

### II. Community Requirements

Before assembling our collection, it is advisable to have some idea of the qualities necessary to each fish before it is admitted to the community, so that fishes which are at present unknown need not be shut out forever from communion with their finny friends because they are not mentioned by name.

In the first place, the fish should be of a social disposition.

39

Some fishes swim in schools of many hundreds of their own kind, but will tear and rend fishes of other species. Such animals, it may be maintained, are social animals, but they do not fit this particular definition of sociablility, and must be ruled out.

Other animals tend to school with others of their own kind, but do not show any animosity to other fishes. Such fishes meet our requirements. Still others are solitary, morose fellows, content to brood over the troubles of the world without benefit of neighbors. If they show no resentment when other fishes intrude on their privacy, they may be included in the family group, but most animals of this nature are unsuitable.

Then there are domineering fishes which set up kingdoms of their own, and destroy with the utmost dispatch any interlopers who, not recognizing boundary lines, may wander to their death. The confines of most household aquaria are less than these despots would choose for their territory, and any fish introduced into the tank will have to fight for his life immediately. These lordly creatures must be banished from the community and given tanks of their own to rule. Many of the Cichlids are of this nature; so the Cichlids as a group are not suitable for fish villages. They are too despotic.

Into the community tank may go those fishes which, while not of a particularly gentle disposition, are limited by nature in the amount of damage they can do. Of this type the Danios are representative, for they have very small mouths and therefore are unable to attack and eat fish more than a quarter of an inch long. They are, however, fond of small fish—particularly of their own young, not in any parental sense, but in a purely gustatorial manner. Still, as the community aquarium is not the place for small fish, the Danios are quite suitable, and indeed are colorful and vivid additions to any aquarium.

Then, of course, fishes which are much larger than the average size—about two inches long—must not be included, for while the individual fish may be entirely peaceful, fishes are inclined to snap up any moving thing as a possible meal. If they don't like it, they release the mouthful, but a fish which is unfortunate enough to find itself in the mouth of another fish has small chance of escaping a speedy death. There are exceptions, of course. Certain catfish will not bother with moving animals, but forage along the bottom of the tank in search of food. These fellows may reach two or three times the size of the average fish in the tank without disastrous results to their neighbors. A few species of catfish are excellent in a tank, for they will take over all the scavenger work, devoting all their waking hours to rooting out and chewing up the smallest scraps of animal or vegetable matter which would otherwise form the nucleus of a fine bacterial colony, with possible tragic results to the population.

Since the healthy, clean, good-looking aquarium is well supplied with plants of one sort or other, it is essential that the proposed inmates should have no desire to destroy the vegetation. It may seem strange, but there are a number of fish which take a vicious delight in ripping up and biting to bits any leaves or stalks of plants that may be near them. The lordly Cichlids are much given to this kind of sabotage, reducing a whole miniature garden of plants to flinders in a few hours. The fish does not eat any of the plants he so ruthlessly destroys, but merely tears them apart and lets them float on the surface. In fact, if the bits are not taken away, he will bite and swirl at the bits of green until they are almost invisibly small pieces. We know of no reason for this destructive urge.

Weatherfish, too, are a nuisance where plants are concerned. These fellows have no objection to the plants, and even like to hang suspended among the leaves. But they also like to dive down into the sand at the bottom and wriggle about there in a fine spirit of playfulness, and it is not a bit good for any plants which may be near, for they will be uprooted and spoiled very quickly. The appearance of the tank and the temper of the owner is not improved by the floating roots continually having to be replaced. Weatherfish, otherwise, are useful members of society, but not that of the community tank. They are much better elsewhere.

## III. Color Variety

For the sake of the good looks of the community, it is necessary to have fishes of a variety of color. Many fishes quite suitable for community life are of a monotonous sameness of livery, usually silver. While they are quite lovely in themselves, sometimes, in some small degree, reflecting all the colors of the spectrum, it is, nevertheless, not very exciting to see a lot of differently shaped fish with the same color. It is much more satisfactory to see several colors, especially as there are so many from which to choose.

One or two silver fish serve well as contrasts to the blues and greens and gold of other fishes, and have their place in the community, but only one or two. For no matter how many fishes of other colors there are in the aquarium, the flashing brightness of moving silver tends to attract and hold the eye, to the loss of the beauty of the community as a whole.

It is interesting to speculate about the reason for all the colors encountered among fishes. The accepted theory of protection does not always seem to work, for while the vast majority of fishes are somewhat dark along the back and have lighter—even white—under parts, there are still large numbers that are speckled and dotted and striped with most spectacular colors which glint and gleam in almost any light. Light and dark fishes are practically invisible from either above or below, and fishes with bars and stripes blend nicely with their surroundings, but some of the others are as obvious as beacons from either top, bottom or side. Fishes which have an unpleasant taste are not infrequently brilliantly hued, but most of our small fishes, which are aquarium animals primarily because of their bright colors, do not appear to have any horrible flavor, for fishes large enough to eat them will do so with relish if they get a chance, as many aquarists know to their sorrow.

If these colors are used for the attraction of the opposite sex during the mating season, there would seem to be no reason why both sexes are similarly colored, even in those species whose colors are heightened and intensified during the spawning, or for the carry-over of the bright colors when the fishes are not mating. However, there are many things to be discovered in nature, and although it is an interesting speculation, we shall not get very far with our present knowledge unless we stay with the fishes which will live together.

There is a fish whose horrific appearance seems to hypnotize its victims into immobility, but neither the colors nor the arrangement—silver and brown, alternating in regular order —seems to have much to do with this effect. Rather, it would appear to be the shape of the beast, which is, from the front, an irregular square, with a gaping mouth at the lower side, and a series of long, waving tentacles, rays of the pectoral fins, all around. This particular fish, the Zebra Fish (*Pterois volitans*), a marine beast from the Indian Ocean, erects all his fins, faces his future meal, and appears to drift toward it. The movement is slow, but the unfortunate Killie destined to be eaten makes no effort to escape, shivering and shaking as if suddenly paralyzed, until the larger fish is within six or seven inches of the Killie, when there is a sudden gulp, and lo, the Killie is no more!

Whatever the reason for the behavior on the part of the marine beast and its subsequent fatal effect on the Killie, most fishes are not built like this eater, although many are colored like him; so we find no gleam of understanding about the reason of these colors in the whole gamut through which they run.

However, for whatever reason the fish disport their fancy colors, we use them as ornaments. That is why we pick out for our community aquarium the most attractively hued fish if they meet all the other requirements.

## IV. Vegetarian Fishes

It is well to include one or two vegetarians in the collection. A properly kept aquarium, with the correct degree of light, will always become the home of some algæ. These are microscopic plants which are always present in ordinary water, and which anchor themselves to the walls of the tank or to any more or less immobile surface. They multiply rapidly and cover the surface with a nice green film, very good for the aquarium, but difficult to see through, and somewhat unsightly. Fortunately, there are one or two fishes which delight in these algæ and will eat quantities of them. These fill all the other requirements; so they may be included in the population as a higher type of scavenger than the Catfish, and one just as important for the beauty of the tank. Indeed, some of these must not be omitted for the sake of their colors.

## V. Platy

The Platyfish is such an animal, and there are no more suitable, colorful or interesting fishes available.

*Platypœcilus maculatus* Guenther called Moonfish or Platy, comes in all colors from a metallic black with a rich blue iridescence, to a pale, washed-out gold. In all of his color manifestations, he eats algae, doesn't fight, doesn't eat or tear the larger plants, is fairly hardy, has interesting breeding habits which he doesn't mind demonstrating if hauled out of the community tank and given a small one for himself, and is altogether lovely. He hails originally from Mexico and Guatemala on the eastward slopes, never having been found on the Pacific side of that narrow strip of land. In his wild haunts he is usually a nondescript mixture of brown and yellow and olive-green, with metallic blue reflections from the rear part of the body. But once in a while a colored animal is discovered.

However, almost all of the fish in our aquaria are of domestic breeding, and the variations achieved by the careful and painstaking selection of stock are varied in the extreme. More than fifty distinct color patterns are now available, although there is a decided preference for clear reds, golds, blues and blacks. All of the varied types will interbreed, and it would not be at all surprising to find many more differently colored animals in the near future, for anyone can develop and fix a new color strain, if he will only take the time and trouble necessary.

The males of this species are smaller than the females, and are not quite so heavily built. They may be distinguished by the stick-like anal fin, held close to the body. The anal fin of the female is large and spread out. The fish is sexually mature when between three and six months old—usually about five—but different specimens and conditions occasion such a spread of time—and the females will deliver broods of from one or two to one hundred and eighty young at a time. The period between broods varies considerably too. An average time of about six weeks between seems to be usual, but as short a time as three weeks, and as long as three months are recorded. As in everything else biological, approximate periods only may be given, for there is always a specimen which does not conform to the mean in such matters to arise and give the lie to him who says it is always thus and so.

## VI. Breeding of Viviparous Fishes

The Platy is a member of the *Pœciliidæ*, a family of fishes which did more to establish tropical fish as pets and ruin the popularity of the goldfish, than all the others combined, although other popular and spectacular fishes were their predecessors in our aquaria by some twenty years. All the members of this family are American, from either tropical or sub-tropical waters, and all live in fresh water, although some are taken from brackish and even wholly salt water. Almost all discovered to date are astonishingly popular, probably because of their remarkable breeding habits, although the ease and rapidity with which they deliver large families of young and the hardiness of those young may have something to do with this.

The sign of the family is that they all have living young, in broods of from one baby to two hundred babies, although all species do not deliver comparable numbers. The anal fin of all the males develops into an intromittent organ, called the "gonopodium" with which the female is fertilized. However, this fertilization is not comparable with that of mammals, for while the fish deliver living young, they are not truly viviparous. The eggs are fertilized within the body of the female parent, but the developing fry are not nourished by her body as in mammals—only by what is in the egg. Just why this should be so is not clearly understood, and the question has been the source of considerable speculation and experimental work, without yielding much in the nature of exact data. A further complication arises from the fact that the females of this family will deliver a number of successive broods—up to six, delivered from three weeks apart—all from the original fertilization. The numbers of the "twins" born at any one time are not consistent throughout the full delivery period, but a curious curve has been observed. The first brood delivered after impregnation is slightly fewer in number than the second, and the third, fourth and fifth fall off in numbers in a regular manner. Those few fish under observation which delivered a sixth brood from one impregnation also showed a steady decrease from the second to the last broods. All of the figures given are averages of a large number of specimens. There are no definite sex complications in the number of young, each brood having both males and females. As a further field for investigation, it has recently been shown that the females of one species in the family are "parthenogenetic," or rather, gynogenetic, that is, the female delivers young in which the male chromosomes have no part in the hereditary mechanism. In other words, all the young are females like their mother.

This facility for changing the parent forms of the *Pœciliidœ* has been the subject of many attempts at crossing the species, but the only successful crosses recorded to date are those of the Platy and a related fish, the Swordtail, and some experimentally successful hybrids from one or two species of *Mollienisia* which we shall talk about later. The first of these crossings has given to the aquarist many beautiful fishes. The Swordtail, a suitable fish for the community tank, if fighting males are excluded, also originates in Mexico and Guatemala, but not in the same river systems from which the Platy comes.

## VII. The Swordtail

This fellow—he has a long, hard name too, *Xiphophorus helleri* Heckel—is somewhat larger than the Platy and much more slender in outline. The color in wild specimens is quite consistent. The upper part of the body is a brownish or bluish green, and the lower, silvery. Along the sides, from the head to the tail, are two lines of a red or yellow-red color. In the male, these lines extend to the extremity of the "sword," a long, pointed projection of the lower part of the tail fin—a projection which names the fish.

The female has no such extension of her tail and the colors are subdued, compared with the males. Breeding behavior is similar to that of the Platy, but the courtship of the female by the male is much more spectacular. The male dashes about the tank madly, trying to catch the eye of the female, and when he thinks he has, he darts back and forth, his body rigid, with the "sword" extended to its maximum. This backward and forward swimming is characteristic of the species, and is a remarkable procedure to watch. The female, which is a little larger than the male—about three inches to his two and a half—usually pays the frenzied male no attention, assuming, or perhaps maintaining, a "don't care" attitude. So, after a period of courting, the male drops all his tactics and concentrates on sneaking up to the female from below or behind! The numbers of young in the broods are similar to those of the Platy, and there is about the same length of time between them.

## VIII. Hybrids

Crosses between these fishes are invariably successful if unfertilized females are used, and there is an approximation in size. And the results are quite interesting. All the colors of the Platyfish are reproduced in the hybrid on a slightly larger scale, and the lines of the Swordtail are still visible. The "sword" however, is usually reduced to a fraction of its former glory, sometimes not even being visible at all or just as a slight point on the tail.

Many of the males of these hybrids are sterile, but the females may usually be bred back to one or the other parent forms. When placing Swordtails in a community aquarium it is advisable to keep all the males under observation for a short while, for these are inclined to fight among themselves, and may hurt some of the other fish.

## IX. Guppies

A related species of fish, the famous Guppy, is also suitable in the community aquarium. This fish, *Lebistes reticulatus* (Peters)—another appalling name for so tiny an animal—seldom reaches a length of two inches, which is about the maximum for the females. The males are only about half as long, but what they lack in size they make up in color, for they are probably the most brilliantly decked-out bits of fish so far discovered. The female is a heavily built, slow-moving, dull grayish-green fish, with a slightly lighter patch of color along the lower margin of the body. But the male, over the same general ground color, is speckled and spotted and barred in all colors of the rainbow. Black, green, blue, yellow, red, purple, orange and all the finer gradations and combinations of these colors may be encountered on the sides of this minute creature, sometimes just one color and sometimes many. It is worthy of note that it is almost impossible to find two males alike, even when the fish are brothers from a long line of closely inbred ancestors. The tails of the male Guppies are the subject of much variation. Fish with one, two, and even three points on their tails are not infrequent, but the usual run of most strains is round- or square-tailed.

Indeed, so well developed are the points of some of the tails of these fish that at one time the fish of this type were thought to be a different kind of Guppy, or a hybrid between Guppy and Swordtail, and were sold as "Swordtail Guppy." However, any male Guppy of any strain may develop a sword, so the breeder of such fish should not be unduly excited if he discovers a fish which he thinks is the result of crossing between this and a related species. As far as has been recorded, there are no crosses of *Lebistes* which develop, although females of related, or even entirely unrelated, species may be fertilized by male Guppy, but the fertilized eggs do not ever result in mongrel fish.

As an instance, the eggs of the ordinary common edible mackerel have been subjected to spermatozoans of Guppy, and fertilization has occurred, as evidence by the expected cell division which took place, but after the first few divisions, the eggs died.

As with the Platy and Helleri, the anal fin of these males develops into the stick-like intromittent organ, by means of which the female is fertilized, and the female produces living babies, but not nearly to the same number that the Platy does. An average of a large number of broods of Guppy was about twenty, although some of the broods were considerably larger. Some females consistently deliver large broods of from thirty to fifty wriggling babies, while others just as consistently deliver small broods of about ten.

In many places about the West Indies, Guppy has been planted as a means of mosquito control. They breed freely under such conditions, and quickly rid any body of water of the larvæ of these pests which spend part of their lives in the water too. Such was the rapidity with which they multiplied that they are well known now as the "Millions Fish," and in our country an ordinary, decently kept aquarium stocked with a few pair of these fish will soon produce enough Guppies to supply the whole neighborhood. This multiplicity of theirs has made the supply a favorite fish for biologists to work with. Much valuable genetic data has been gathered by keeping accurate records of the kinds of young produced by the matings of these fish of different strains and color patterns, data which may be gathered from the records of the characteristics of almost any animal or plant, but which, with other animals, would take infinitely longer to assemble, for outside of animals without a backbone—the difference between large groups of animals is the lack or possession of a backbone—there is hardly an animal which takes to captivity so well and breeds at such short intervals.

These Guppy produce their first brood when they are about three months old, the fish from the fifth and sixth broods of the initial fertilization frequently being great-uncles before they are born. Foolish as this sounds, it may be easily demonstrated, for broods are born at about twenty-eight-day intervals, and if a female is segregated as the delivery of the first brood approaches and the broods kept in separate containers, the first brood will be delivering broods of their own when the third or fourth brood of their brothers and sisters are being born, and these grandchildren of the original parent will be delivering young at about the same time that the fifth or sixth brood of their grandmothers is being delivered. This is, of course, pretty close estimating, but it has been recorded many times, especially when the females are of a strain which bear at an early age. (Strains in fish vary. Some will be sexually mature when others, kept at a lower temperature, perhaps, or undernourished by improper feeding, are still adolescents.)

## X. "Mollies"

The next fish of this family suitable for community life is the subject of much misunderstanding. Some of them are true salt-water fish, but since they live along the coasts and are frequently caught in tide pools which are filled with fresh water in a heavy rain, they have developed the ability to live in both fresh and salt water. They are a rather large fish, compared with their close relatives of the family, but are very peaceful and will eat the tiny green plants, the algæ, which grow in fresh water, with complete enjoyment and thorough health. These are the Mollienisas, a genus of fishes found from the coastal waters of Florida to the fresh streams of Mexico and Guatemala. One or two species are well known, the others not so well known.

The best known is the Mud Pusser of Florida, a fish which is losing place to its decadent descendant, the Black Mollie. Incidentally, all of these fishes are known as "Mollies." This black fellow is a very beautiful velvety black in the best specimens. He is suffering from a maladjustment of his color cells, in which the black chromatophores—the cells in the skin which contain the coloring matter—grow to the exclusion of any other color. There are various stages of this melanosis, as it is called. In one of the stages, there are merely a few black spots; in others, the major portion of the body is black, with a few whitish areas scattered about, and in the most prized specimens, there is not a bit of any color but black to be seen. These black fish lose one of their recommendations to aquarists when they become black, for most of the huge development of the dorsal fin, a feature which was originally the chief source of appeal to the heart of the good fish keeper, disappears. In old normal males, the dorsal fin is sometimes so large that the fish cannot carry it erect, but swims about with it draped in graceful folds across the body. The females lack this gorgeous finny decoration, but they are generally larger than their mates and of a much more placid disposition.

The wild green *Mollienisia latipinna,* as the Mud Pusser label reads when he is kept in glass bottles in museums, reaches four inches in length when he is taken in the sea, but fishes of this size seldom become reconciled to tank life and are rarely seen in aquaria. Smaller fish, born in the wild, however, will live very nicely in a small tank of fresh water, but they show their appreciation of the addition of a little salt, even table salt, by growing faster and donning a more brilliant uniform. The fin of the male may reach one inch in height and two in length, and has frequently caused the fish to be mistaken for his relative *Mollienisia velifera,* of Yucatan, and much more rare in aquaria. This fellow is the real sailfin, if ever there was one, for his dorsal fin is much bigger than his body as often as not.

However, let's stay with *Mollienisia latipinna* until we have disposed of him and the black phase. In nature black fishes sometimes occur, but they are so easily picked out by predatory animals that few if any really achieve maturity. Most of the species are a greenish olive, with lines of blue and red spots on the scales all over the body. In addition, the male has several bars across the body. The dorsal is well colored, as becomes its large size. The basic color is blue, with lines of deeper blue, green and reddish spots along it, and an orange margin. The female is more demurely colored, with only small spots of a color not easily determined. The tails of each fish fit well with the general color scheme of the other fins. The melanistic form is smaller than the colored brethren and is jet black in the best specimens.

Perhaps because of the lack of salt water, the breeding of these fish in captivity is erratic. Females are recorded which have delivered broods of more than one hundred living babies at intervals of about one month, while there are other females, apparently in just as good health, which have only delivered ten or fifteen youngsters every three months or so. Any variation of these figures seem to be quite normal. Fishes of the black phase seem to share the others' dislike of being classified by breeding in a similarly erratic manner, but in consistently lower numbers. The practice usually followed by aquarists of transferring gravid females of this family to uninhabited aquaria to deliver their young is fraught with the utmost risk in this case. Fishes moved in such a condition usually deliver the babies prematurely, with the attendant risk to the mother, and almost sure death to the young. However, there is a consoling feature for the aquarist. If he really wishes to breed such fish, he may place a pair together and leave them, with a tolerably fair chance that any young born to them will not be eaten, for the fish is primarily a vegetarian and only eats animal foods under pressure of starvation.

*Mollienisia velifera,* mentioned before, is only suitable as a community animal when he is not fully grown, for he is quite bad-tempered, and will kill other fishes even when he has no intention of eating them. However, as he is practically unknown to all but specialists, we will not discuss him except to say that he is a paler version of the well-known Mollie, but differentiated by the larger fin, and the number of rays in it.

Ray counts are one of the methods of identification used by ichthyologists. The rays are the gristly supports of fish fins, and our Mollie has only fourteen or fifteen rays, while *Mollienisia velifera* never has fewer than eighteen.

Quite frequently a fish called *Mollienisia sphenops* is mentioned by aquarists, especially when they are talking of the Black Mollie. *Sphenops* is quite suitable for community life, being peaceful and of a certain degree of usefulness, for he will eat a certain amount of algæ and thus help to keep the tank clean. He is almost unknown to science as a domestic fish, but scientists are, by reputation, dry-as-dust anyway, and seem to be used only in the last extremity by the aquarist; so we will include this fellow in our discussion long enough to say that he is similar to *Mollienisia latipinna* in size, almost as variable as the Guppy in color, much less striking in general appearance than either of the other two Mollies mentioned. He also has a tendency to melanism, which is the chief cause of the confusion in names, for many black or spotted Mollies are offered as *Mollienisia sphenops.* He comes from both sides and the middle of Central America, from fresh, brackish, or salt water, and from the Leeward Islands. This is one of the fishes which give rise to the newly discovered theory of gynogenetism in fishes, for males of this species mate with and stimulate females of another species of Mollie, equally rare in aquaria, without ever passing on to their offspring any of their own characteristics. The fishes thus produced are always females, and are temporarily labeled as *Mollienisia formosa,* the females of which species are old acquaintances of ichthyologists without a male ever having appeared! The other fish which produces *Mollienisia formosa* when cross-mated is the old reliable *Mollienisia latipinna.*

I hope my readers will not be irritated with me for using so many names, but without using them, I don't know how to straighten out the scrambled nomenclature in the minds of the aquarists who are always wondering which is which.

## XI. Anableps

A very curious fish of a family closely related to all these live-bearing fishes is *Fitzroyia lineata,* a creature whose habitat extends from the Rio Grande do Sul to La Plata. Fitzroyia—it has no common name because it is somewhat rare in domestic tanks, but is included here because there are a number of expeditions looking for it and it will probably become popular if anyone brings in a few—is the only fresh-water species of the family to which *Anableps*—the four-eyed fish—belongs which is in any way suitable for aquarium life.

The family is very odd; the fishes have a peculiar eye, split in the middle. As they swim along the surface, they keep part of the head out of water—just sufficient to expose half the eye. The upper half of this organ is constructed to see in air; the lower to see in water. The four eyes are, therefore, only two in reality, but each does double duty. Our fresh-water fish, however, does not have this fancy eye arrangement, but he does have the characteristic breeding structures.

This fish delivers living babies, but not every male can mate with every female. Over the genital pore of all the females is a sort of flap attached to the side. Some females have this on the left side; some have it on the right, and since the male has a similar adjustment on the gonopodium which only allows it to be turned to one side, either right or left, a male whose intromittent organ points to the right is unable to fertilize a female who has the flap on the left, and vice versa. There does not seem to be any reason for this, for the young of each female—there are as many as thirty in a brood—are apparently left- or right-sided individuals merely by chance. It would be disastrous to the species as a whole if all the males happened to be born left-sided and the females likewise, for then there would be no fertilized females to carry on, and the species would disappear.

The fish is bluish, with five brown stripes along the body. Both sexes are alike in this, but the males are much smaller than the females—about one and a half inches to four inches of female, and the femâle lacks the tube-like development of the anal fin. If they ever get into the stores, the aquarist is going to have a lot of fun swapping all his mismated fish for others more suitable.

## XII. Limias

There are a lot of Limias in the family of live-bearing fish, but with the exception of one or two, they are more or less unknown outside the tanks of very expert aquarists, and many of them have not yet arrived in popular favor at all, because none of them is particularly colorful and their breeding behavior is more or less duplicated by the Platies and the Mollies.

There is one, however, which has a very *outré* shape, and which makes a bid for attention every little while. This is the Black-banded Limia, *Limia nigrofasciata*. The fish comes from Haiti—it is interesting to note that the long string of islands extending from Florida to Venezuela is a very poor hunting ground for fresh-water fishes, although their marine fishes compare favorably in numbers, color and odd behavior with any other in the world—and the old males develop a very decided "hump" on their backs. Their snouts being pushed forward, they present a very definite "dish-face" in profile. This little fellow is a dull brownish-green color, with a number of dark lines across the body, and a blue sheen reflected from him when he is viewed in certain lights. He breeds easily in numbers and periods comparable with the Platy, and neither the young nor females show any tendency to a "hump-back."

All of the Limias come from the islands, none has ever been recorded from the American mainland, and while they are sufficiently unlike to warrant different specific names, they are still near enough in structure to be classed together in the same genus. Perhaps they are all descendants of the original Limia, forced by their different environments to adapt themselves in color and size to some peculiarity of the island homes, but it is difficult to visualize any environment which calls for such a hump on the back of the elderly males of this particular species under discussion. However, we shall leave the Limias to themselves and talk about more interesting fishes.

## XIII. Mosquito Fish

The business of making records of the largest or smallest of something or other is extended to fishes. Many journals periodically list the largest this or the smallest that, or the heaviest something else in the fish world. This is not confined to game fish or food fish or whales or sharks. Until recently one of our small Pœciliids carried on his tiny back the distinction of being the smallest fish in the world. When another fish was discovered in the Philippines to be smaller than our little fellow, the distinction of being the smallest fish in the world was taken from him, and that of being the smallest viviparous vertebrate given in exchange.

This tiny creature, a native of our own North American waters, is *Heterandria formosa,* and the males are little, if any, longer than the second part of their name. The females are somewhat larger, and they are really a little too small to go into the community aquarium, for a good-sized female Guppy is large enough to go into Heterandria's mythology as the giantess who eats all bad Mosquito Fish, as they are called for short.

Anyway, Heterandria is a modestly dressed, peaceful little fish which is quite content to live in the smallest of small aquaria, and will produce the smallest living fish you can possibly imagine. The female of this fish differs from her relatives because she only delivers one baby at a time. Sometimes her brood will number twenty or so, but they are released from her body at the rate of about one, or perhaps two, a day, until the whole brood is born. Then she takes about a month before she starts delivering the next brood. New-born babies are scarcely longer than one-eighth of an inch and are about as thick and wide as a medium-sized horse hair. In spite of their small size, they are quite ferocious when it comes to feeding. In a natural state they will eat only living things, and they have to be accustomed to a diet of canned fish food. Many of their larger relatives, it will be remembered, are content to graze on the microscopic green plants which grow in their tanks. However, in a tank of one gallon capacity, a family of Heterandria will grow nicely, for there is enough space for the babies to hide from the jaws of papa and mamma. Incidentally, almost all of these fishes will eat their own children under pressure, but the pressure, not well understood by the average aquarist who often thinks his fish have stopped breeding, is unwittingly applied by the fish themselves which increase in numbers until the capacity of the tank is reached. Any babies born thereafter are consigned to the interior immediately. Individual specimens, of course, reach an age when breeding is impossible, but I mean that the whole tankful of fish are often accused of lying down on the job when all they are doing is eating whatever babies may be born the second they appear. In experiments it was found that this was good sense on the part of the older fish, for when they missed a few babies, who in a day or so learned that they had to hide if they wanted to live, the younger fish soon grew so that their greater agility crowded out the older, slower fish in the scramble for food, and then the elders of the family died.

Nevertheless, Heterandria, are interesting little fish and may be kept where lack of space forbids keeping fish that require larger quarters.

## XIV. Belonesox

A fish of the same family which must on no account be placed with other fishes is *Belonesox belizanus*. This fellow has no popular name for he is not popular with the average aquarist, because he is so hard to feed. He will eat only living food, just as his tiny relative Heterandria, but his larger size, four or five times larger in the case of the male and about eight times larger in the female, and the ugly, long, beak-like mouth, make him almost impossible to fill with Guppies or similar animals. While not quite as bad as some deep-sea fishes which eat other fishes larger than themselves, the Belonesox will eat a tremendous amount of fish. Some of them about five inches long ate as many as three salmon fingerlings nearly as long as themselves at one meal, and were quite ready to tackle others later in the same day. It is no wonder that a fish fancier who unwittingly acquires some of these beasts soon gets rid of them. It usually transpires that one keeps half a dozen tanks of ordinary fish merely as breeding grounds for the food of a pair of the Belonesox, and still the Belonesox will be half starved.

The fish delivers young alive—about forty hungry mouths at a time—although not many people who have tried to keep the creatures have succeeded in raising any of them, probably because they are so everlastingly hungry and usually one half satisfied.

How fishes eat such comparatively large meals is not hard to understand, but how they get such large bits of food into their mouths is not at once apparent. If a pair of these fishes is watched, it will be noticed that they first catch their dinner anywhere—wherever they can seize best the uncannily fast swoop they make on the unfortunate fish, and then sort of edge it up until the head of the wriggling animal is in their jaws. Then the whole mouth seems to stretch out. The jaws are distended in all directions, for they are not locked in place by bony joints as ours are, but are held together by tough, flexible tissue. And the fish meal just slides out of sight. Its progress down the gullet, if it is fairly large, and into the stomach is quite easily discernible.

For all its ugliness, the mouth of Belonesox does not appear as vicious as it really is. The horrible sharp teeth are covered with a sort of lip until the fish reaches old age and the lip loses its tautness and falls away from the jaws, making the creature's appearance so much more nightmarish by the addition of long fleshy flaps pendant from each side of the jaw.

The babies of this fellow are quite large in proportion to the size of the mother. They are about an inch long, a fact which stimulated one inquiring person to investigate the method by which they are packed before they are released by the mother. He reported that they were laid out in a compact group, the head of one next the tail of the next, like a can of sardines! If this is so, it is the most remarkable way of carrying young so far reported. But it is unlikely, for the fish first start from eggs, and the straightening out they would have to do after the cover of the shell is ruptured would call for an unreasonable amount of backing and filling, backing and filling for which there is very little room.

Do not ever turn a Belonesox loose with other fish, not even with his own wife, unless he has lived with her for a long time. Either she will eat him, or he will eat everything else available! Like a spider, Madame Belonesox will eat her husband if nothing better offers, and when she is hungry, which is always, husband and wife will become one in bitter earnest one fine night. Like acute indigestion, many fish strike each other at night or during the early morning.

# Chapter 6

## The Carp Family

### I. Distribution

WE HAVE rambled on at great length about the viviparous fishes. There are others.

In popularity, the second prize-winning family is that of the Goldfish. Not the Goldfish themselves, but their smaller, more colorful relatives. This family has a tremendous number of species. They range all over the known world, with the possible exception of Australasia and a few of the oceanic islands, and are to be found in waters of all temperatures, from the thermal springs of Ceylon to the ice-cold waters of British Columbia. They do not, however, extend in any great variety far south of the Rio Grande. However, in that region their place is taken by the Characins, a closely related family, and, according to some authorities, the parent family of the Carps, the popular name by which the family is commonly known.

The popular tropical fishes, however, are mainly from Southern Asia and Africa. One of the absolute requirements of home aquarium fishes is that they must be able to live in the warm waters of a household aquarium, and cold-water fishes, while they may be adapted to human habitations, require more water than is often convenient, and so are relatively unknown as domestic pets.

The Goldfish in all its manifestations is the exception, being an exceedingly popular and abused cold-water animal.

### II. Barbs

There are many genera in this family, the Cyprinidæ, but the largest, as far as we are concerned, is the genus *Barbus*. There are probably at least one thousand species of Barbs on record from the East Indies, north and west through Southern Europe to Africa, and there is a very considerable difference in size between members of the genus. Specimens of the largest have been captured weighing about one hundred pounds; these are, for obvious reasons, not aquarium fishes. But the small species by far outnumber the larger ones, and most of the small ones are suitable for domestic aquaria. They are not particularly attractive creatures, nor do they have any interesting habits, so they have never made much headway, as a group, into the affections of the aquarist, who must find one or other of these virtues in each fish before he will consider it seriously. Another drawback is the difficulty of distinguishing between the sexes of the various species. Almost all of the Asiatic Barbs carry the marks of their sex where they may be easily discerned by the fish-keeper. But almost none of the Africanders is so obliging. The European fishes are not considered because they are not very suitable for the warm water of our aquaria, and are almost unknown outside of strictly scientific circles. This difference in sex of the Asians perhaps accounts for the balance of popularity in the family being in their favor, for very few African Barbs are known to the fish fanciers, but occasionally a few drift into America and are finally lost in the darkest tanks where unwanted fishes go.

## III. Breeding of Barbs

All, or almost all, of the Barbs scatter adhesive eggs in clusters of close-leaved plants, to which the eggs stick during the incubation period of one or two days. There is no parental care, and it is not unusual for the parent fishes to devour the eggs as soon as they are deposited. However, by the observation of a few simple rules, and a little care, large numbers of these fish may be obtained by anyone interested enough to try for them. A fairly large aquarium—say, not less than five gallons, and larger than that if possible—should be filled with good aquarium water. A few stalks of such plants as Cabomba, Myriophyllum or Utricularia minor should be rooted either in sand at the bottom of the tank, or in pots or saucers of pebbles, and a pair of fish introduced. Two males to each female may be successfully used, but this is not essential. After the fish have spawned, either the fish, or the plants, should be taken out and placed in another aquarium. If the spawning was successful, the plants will soon be alive with tiny fishes which must then be looked after as all small fishes are looked after. It is always advisable to give the eggs as large a tank as possible so that the growing youngsters will not crowd each other out before they are large enough to be moved.

The courtship of these animals consists almost entirely of a long chase of the female by the male, and a series of very close circles by the pair, during which the eggs are liberated.

This breeding behavior is common to all the Barbs at present in our aquaria. It only remains now to indicate some of the names, and the signs by which fish ready to spawn may be recognized.

Besides the difference in color, if any, the female is usually deeper in the body in all of these species, and sometimes a little longer from head to tail.

## IV. Rosy Barb

The first Barb usually acquired by the aquarist is the Rosy Barb of the Northwestern Provinces of India and Bengal. His full name is *Barbus conchonius*, and, as his popular name indicates, he is a rosy color. This, however, is only true of old males or at spawning time and only along the lower part of the sides. The females retain a demure olive-brown uniform, enlivened by a round black spot at the base of the tail.

## V. Golden Barb

A somewhat rare Barb is the Golden Barb of Bengal and Central India, *Barbus gelius*. There is a substantial difference in the size of the sexes. The female is about two inches long, one-third again as long as the male. These fishes are golden, both sexes the same color. While well worth a place in any aquarium, we see them but seldom.

## VI. Iridescent Barb

A fish much more in the popular fancy is the Iridescent Barb, *Barbus oligolepis*, of Sumatra, of about the same size as the Golden Barb. The sexes have distinctive markings although they are of approximately the same size. The male is much more colorful than the female and has black edges on the dorsal and anal fins, which his mate lacks.

## VII. Swamp Barb

Somewhat larger and at one time more popular than either of the last two species is the Swamp Barb, *Barbus chola*. This fellow may reach five inches, but is usually smaller. Both sexes carry two dark spots, one under the fore part of the dorsal fin, and one near the tail. These spots are much lighter in the female than in the male, who is generally more highly colored anyway.

## VIII. Miscellaneous Barbs

A Barb from China will relieve me of saying India so often. We have one, the Half-banded Barb, with an impressively long scientific name, *Barbus semifasciolatus*. Many of the common names, if you notice, are merely translations of scientific names. This fellow is a greenish fish of about two inches or a little longer. There are a series of six thin dark lines across the body, and as breeding time approaches, the male assumes a fine red color, especially along the underpart of the body. The sexes are alike except for the ruddiness, but after one or two peeps at a pair of these animals, even an inexperienced eye can distinguish male from female.

Similar to this fish in many respects is the banded barb, *Barbus fasciolatus*. This fish has about twelve dark lines across his body, and comes from Central West Africa. He is reported specifically from Angola, but probably gets over the borders of that country a bit.

*Barbus trispilus* (three-spotted) is from the same part of the world—the Cameroons—but he is not common in aquaria. Another rare Barb from the same and adjacent countries is a pretty yellow fish, about three inches long, with an orange and white dorsal fin. His name, *Barbus callipterus,* as usual does not roll readily off the tongue, but we could easily overlook that if there were more of him in our tanks.

Just to diversify our African Barbs, we shall include the Algerian Barb, *Barbus setivimensis,* a nice-looking copper-colored fish from Northwestern Africa, just about where the French Foreign Legion holds forth. Normally, he is quite a large fish—about twelve inches—but aquarium specimens, of which there are a few available, are not above two or three inches long. The young are usually spotted for a few months after birth.

*Barbus unitæniatus* comes from Zululand and points thereabouts—his name suggests some such origin and means, roughly, that he has one stripe. He is a small person compared with the other Africanders, only between two and three inches long when full grown, and not very colorful, mostly brown.

Two fairly big fellows from the East Indian Archipelago, and we're done with the Barbs. The first, *Barbus binotatus* (with two spots), has caused some trouble about his identification on his infrequent appearances in North America, for the two spots vary considerably in their location on the sides of different specimens. He is large, about seven inches long, and is not usually suited for community life. The next is even larger —about an inch larger—and very handsome. He is orange or greenish gold in color, with a sort of dark saddle mark on his back and sides, another dark splotch beneath the gill cover and one or two stripes on his sides. Both sexes are alike, so it's not much use trying to pick them out. This one is called *Barbus lateristriga*.

With such a large group of fishes as the Barbs comprise, it is almost impossible to keep pace with new ones that are continually being discovered. For the reason given when we started on the genus, we are not going to include any more of them here, for it is doubtful if any new one will make much headway with aquarists for a while. So we will go on to some other members of the Carp family.

## IX. The "Danios"

A fish popularly allied with the Brachydanios, usually called "Danios" in error, is *Danio malabaricus*. Because he has been so mistaken, he gets a paragraph of his own.

He is a fairly large fish from the southwestern coast of India and Ceylon. His name indicates the locality and he is the only true Danio we have. He is quite lovely and very active. His colors are a steely blue on the back, with a rosy pink belly. Three or four blue stripes run from his shoulder to the tail. In the male, the straight blue tail stripe is margined above and below with yellow. In the female this blue stripe slants upward to the margin of the tail-fin, and there is no yellow. Between the blue stripes of the body, on both sexes, there is a yellow tinge, making as nice-looking a fish as one could wish for. Good specimens sometimes run four inches long. This fish breeds in a manner similar to the Barbs and about as freely, after the trick of keeping it is once acquired.

The group in which *Danio malabaricus* is often included is closely related and is known as the "Danios," although they are really Brachydanios. There are three species in the genus, all exceedingly popular, small fellows, available in almost any pet store. The first is the zebra fish, *Brachydanio rerio*, originally from Bengal, Madras and adjoining regions of India, but for many years bred in domestic aquaria in Europe and America. This fish has a very even pattern of silver and blue stripes from head to tail. So evenly is he marked that there seems to be no definite striping or body color. The stripes are continuous on the anal fin, a remarkable occurrence in fish patterns. In addition to the two major colors, the lower part of the body of the male is shaded with lemon yellow. The whole color scheme is attractive in the extreme.

His near Sumatran relative, *Brachydanio albolineatus*, is popularly called the Pearl Danio because of his similarity in color to the pearly reflections of some shells. The movements of this fish as well as those of its related species are so rapid that an analysis of the color pattern is difficult. The basic tint of the Pearl Danio is a blue or green, shading toward the top of the body. There is a bright scarlet and violet line running down the body, widening out on the tail. The whole appearance is a kaleidoscopic blending of blues, violets and pinks, fascinating to watch. There are also, on the male's anal fin, three fine lines of blue, red and green. The female has to be content with a yellowish-green anal fin.

Of somewhat less popularity than either of the other two Brachydanios is the third, *Brachydanio analipunctatus*, from Burma. He resembles the Pearl Danio, except that he has another line of dark dots below all the others, and reaching to the end of the tail, and the male's anal fin is edged with gold.

All of the Brachydanios are small, about two inches long, and all are gentle creatures. The first two spawn freely in clear tanks over a pebbly bottom, and they will all spawn anywhere. But if there are not a lot of crevices to receive the eggs, they will be eaten immediately. A layer of rather small stones on the bottom of the tank provides the necessary crannies, and the fish should be removed after spawning, if any fry are to be saved.

The eggs take about two days to hatch, but sometimes a few infants are out in one day, and sometimes not for three days. Besides the differences in color, all the females are much more heavily built than the males, and the lower outline of their body is distinctly convex.

The last one, the Spotted Danio, does not spawn as freely as its two cousins, which is probably why it is not so popular.

Various tricks have been resorted to to make these fish spawn, the most successful being to add fresh *cool* water to the aquarium late in the evening. But unless the fish are healthy, they cannot spawn, and if they are healthy, they will spawn in spite of anything anyone does to stop them.

However, if the aquarist sees any undue activity among his Danios, he should isolate the excessively active ones for a while and then bring them together in an aquarium with a gravelly bottom, for it does the soul of the most sophisticated fish-keeper good to have his fish spawn in the place he designates, and gives him something to crow over when he has raised a spawning of fish to a successful maturity.

## X. Flying Nuria

Once in a great while a relative of the Danios pops up in the aquarium stores. This is the Flying Nuria, *Esomus danricus*. It is a little larger than the largest of the Danios, and comes from substantially the same area, but with a supposedly larger range, being doubtfully reported from the Malay States as well as India. The name, Flying Nuria, really a misnomer, alludes to the long leaps the fish can make, balancing and possibly supporting itself on the very much enlarged pectoral fins. This fellow likes to bask in the sun and seems to have a decided preference for heat, for it is in the habit of making its way toward the sources of hot springs. This fish is not particularly attractive and does not breed well in aquaria, so it has not found much favor except as a novelty. But in case anyone should be sufficiently interested to raise it, the eggs are slightly adhesive, and are deposited among water plants, where they hatch in about three days. The fish is brownish-green on top and silvery below, with a line of dark brown or black along the flanks, terminating in a spot at the base of the tail. Both sexes are alike, but occasionally both line and spot are missing in the female.

A variation of this species, or an entirely different one (it is not definitely known whether there are two species or two races of one species), with identical habits and the addition of a silver line along the body to the end of the tail, comes from the region about Calcutta, India. This fish has been called *Esomus lineatus*, and is still less frequently encountered than the other.

## XI. The Rasboras

Much more attractive than *Esomus*, and of exceeding popularity, is *Rasbora*. There are many fishes in this genus, but most of them are unknown, or are completely put in the shade by the glory of the brilliant Red Rasbora, *Rasbora heteromorpha*. This fish, from the Malay Peninsula, and thereabouts, is fairly small, hardly reaching two inches in length, but it is more colorful than any of its relatives and is of the most peaceable disposition. The general body color is greenish, with red reflections. A large black or blue-black triangle covers most of the body between the dorsal, anal and caudal fins. A red and gold horizontal line is evident between the upper point of the triangle and the dorsal fin, which is a deep, rich red. The anal fin is red too, and both fins are tipped with black. It is difficult to distinguish sex, but besides the fact that the body of the male is slimmer than that of the female, he is more brilliantly colored, and the triangle and gold line are somewhat larger and longer respectively.

Breeding this fish is interesting and is quite an achievement if one is sufficiently fortunate to have it happen in the aquarium. They apparently like to mate in groups, although each pair acts independently of the others. The female selects a suitable leaf, which must be fairly stiff, and deposits a row of eggs on the under side. The eggs are arranged closely, and sometimes two rows run together for about two inches. Then the male fertilizers them, and the fishes go off to another leaf and repeat the procedure. The eggs hatch in about four days.

These fish have been bred only once or twice in American aquaria, in spite of numberless attempts to encourage the breeding on the part of aquarists. But since they have been bred at all, there is no reason why care and patience in the arrangement of really suitable aquaria should not result in more young Rasboras.

There are other Rasboras, but they are infrequent visitors to our shores, and have never captured the acclaim the Red Rasbora receives. Possibly this is due to their unresponsiveness to attempts to breed them, which is very discouraging to good aquarists. And since they very often lose their brilliant colors in captivity, the fish-fanciers as a group have a common apathy toward them.

Strangely enough, there is a Rasbora called the Brilliant Rasbora, which is not the Red Rasbora and has not his lovely colors, although it is really a very lovely fish. However, its blues, reds and greens are not as well marked as in its relative, and the general effect is one of pallor. This fish also comes from the Malay Peninsula. It is known scientifically as *Rasbora einthoveni*, and is only about twice as large as *Rasbora heteromorpha*, which it resembles in its lack of sexual differentiation. *Rasbora maculata*, the Spotted Rasbora, is very tiny, little more than an inch long. It comes from Malacca and is supposed to be another form of *Rasbora kalachroma* from Sumatra and Borneo, but it is so rare in aquaria, I think we need say no more about it.

The Yellow Rasbora, *Rasbora elegans*, is more common than most of the others, but still scarce in aquaria. It is yellow, with a red back and white ventral area. It comes from the Malay States and the adjacent islands, and grows to five inches. A peculiar development of the tail is worthy of note. The lower lobe of the tail fin of the male is larger than the upper lobe, but whether or not this has any significance is un-known.

*Rasbora daniconius* is sometimes offered for sale by well-stocked pet shops, but it is at best only an occasional visitor to North America. However, it is quite a good-looking fish, orna-mental in a somewhat lesser degree than the Red Rasbora. The general body color is pink or green; many of these fish show alternate colors which flash in view according to the angle from which they are observed, and which fade in death so that there is no real definitiveness about a color description of such fish. But there is no mistaking the metallic blue line which runs from the eye to the tail in this fish, even if it is indicated only by a row of dots or dashes instead of being complete and solid. This fish is about five inches long, and comes from eastern India.

While there are many, many more fishes in this family, the vast majority of them are entire strangers to our aquaria and have no place in such a volume as this. Many of the casual visitors, too, have no place here, for they rarely leave the hands of specialists in such animals who have their own literature, which is specialized and tedious reading, except to the more or less technically minded. And such people rarely keep fishes at home for pleasure.

Chapter 7

## The Characins

I MENTIONED previously that the Characins almost wholly usurp the place of the otherwise world-wide Carps in South America. This is a curious family. It is a fairly large one with most of its representatives in Central and South America, and a few in Africa.

There are about fifty species of Characins available at one time or other in fish stores, most of them suitable for community tanks, but since the majority of them are so much alike that they are impossible to identify in life—and aquarists are not interested in dead fishes—only the most popular ones with their oustanding characteristics will be mentioned here.

### I. Breeding Habits

Most of the Characinidæ deposit adhesive eggs in masses of leaves and stalks of plants. The eggs are usually unattended and hatch in one, two or three days, but there are a few cases of specialized breeding behavior which we shall mention as we come to the fish.

### II. The Piranhas

The family Characinidæ includes such peaceful little fellows as the "Head and Tail Light," and such horribly vicious beasts as the Piranhas, made famous, or rather infamous, by President Theodore Roosevelt in his description of the River of Doubt.

There are to date between twenty and thirty species of fish known as Piranha, all small and all equally bloodthirsty. None of them is recorded as over eighteen inches or thereabouts, and several of them are only about six inches long when full grown, but they all show an appalling and amazing ability and readiness to destroy other animals. Nothing is safe from their ferocious jaws and from the sharp teeth which are usually hidden behind innocent enough lips. They will rend and tear flesh until there is only a skeleton left, biting off the tissue in large pieces which they immediately drop after their hunger is appeased. Cases are recorded where a swarm of them has reduced living cattle to a heap of bones in fifteen or twenty minutes. They are not at all pleasant fishes to keep in aquaria, even if they should become generally available. The hand that feeds them is just as acceptable to them as their intended meal.

These savage beasts are seldom available for the private collector's tanks, but once in a while a few arrive at one or other port and are eagerly snapped up as a novelty by an ardent fish fancier. If any are procured, the greatest care should be exercised in handling them, for they are not in the least bashful about biting, and even a small one of two or three inches will take quite a piece out of a hand. They should not be placed with other fishes, of course, for unless the tank is very large, they will not tolerate any invasion of their territory, and their territory is any in which they happen to find themselves. Some specimens have been kept in tanks in which small Swordtails and Platies were growing. The small fish were never molested, but as they grew to a size large enough to attract the eye of His Majesty the Piranha, he dined off them without further ado. This idea that he is monarch of all he surveys is common to each and every one, so it is even impossible to keep two of the same species together unless they are breeding, a most unlikely happening, for the few fishes ever brought into this country are all immature specimens and have to be kept until they are at least sexually of age. The odds against finding a pair of these fishes which show no sexual differentiation, keeping them until they are ready to spawn, and then successfully introducing them into the same aquarium without disaster to one or both, are enormous. However, they are interesting fish whose tooth marks in a piece of tough beef will be a source of pride to their owner.

From all of which you should gather that the Piranhas are *not* community aquarium fishes! If any are procured, it is not even safe to leave them together, for they fight ferociously among themselves. Three specimens I had in my care were left together for a while. Eventually two of them attacked the third, and in a few minutes he was scattered about the tank. Remarkably enough, though, his head and entrails were intact and although there was not more than one-third of his body left, the mouth was still biting hard, and as he was being lifted from the tank, the jaws seized on the tweezers and held on with a grip difficult to dislodge. He died, of course!

The usual genus to appear this far north is *Serrasalmo,* of which there are several species. These are almost indistinguishable one from the other in life, the standard means of identifying such animals being the scale count; that is, the number of scales along the lateral line, or above or below it, or by the body proportions and number and position of the teeth—a quest no one in his right mind would undertake with live specimens of such little snappers.

Several closely related genera are sometimes known as Piranhas too. Some species of these are quite frequently encountered among the inhabitants of the well-stocked aquarists' tanks, but they are rather expensive and rare, and only the greatest subscribers to the hobby usually bother with them. *Metynnis maculatus,* the Spotted Piranha, is one of these. This is a fish of about eight inches when full grown, and is not quite as savage as some of the fishes related to him. At least, he will not destroy at sight everything else in the tank, but he does not like plants very much, biting and tearing at the stalks until the plant is destroyed. He also is not particularly good-looking, being of rather squarish shape and a yellowish color, with brown spots on his side. The fins are dark, almost black, and there is little or no difference between the sexes. Another of this type is *Metynnis roosevelti,* a little larger than *metynnis maculatus,* and darker in color. It still has the spots though, but the fins are lightly touched with a reddish-yellow shade. He is a little prettier than his relative, and is of the same general habits.

Nothing is known with any certainty of such fishes' breeding habits. If they are like those of the vast majority of the family of Characins, they will just drop their eggs about in plants, but since they show the strongest aversion to plants of any sort, even floating ones, it is possible that they place their eggs in a depression in the sand at the bottom of the water and take some care of them. The destruction of plants would indicate the possibility of this method, for plants would provide good cover for any animal that might relish the eggs and might be snooping around waiting to snatch a mouthful; so the fish, taking no chances, and not finding a place in the aquarium without plants, clears them all out. This action, if it may be called an action, would not run counter to the theories of those who will not admit any possibility of fishes showing evidence of sense. For if the baby fishes are born into a plantless world, neat and tidy with all the stones and bits of sand in place, they would be so conditioned that they would not want any plants about and would take the necessary steps to get rid of them, not through any process of reasoning but because such things had never been before in their lives, and they are not going to change things now.

However, no one has ever offered any evidence of the spawning of such fishes, so we must perforce omit any description of that phenomenon.

### III. The Brown Characin

Another of the nasty Characins is the Brown Characin, *Hoplias malabaricus,* which ranges over most of Northeastern South America. This fish is valued as a food fish in its native haunts. It grows to almost two feet long and has the unpleasant habit of "lying doggo" until a school of Bloodfins passes by, when he dashes into them, biting and swallowing dozens. He also is not an aquarium fish, but is mentioned because occasional small specimens arrive here and are sold by unsuspecting dealers who are unacquainted with his habits to ardent aquarists whose eagerness for new fish exceeds their knowledge.

One case reported recently was that two of these fishes had been sold as Carnegiellas. The cautious purchaser, not liking the look of their jaws, inquired if Carnegiella were safe to put with other fish. Having been assured that they were, he added these to his very large community aquarium, and lost almost all of his prized pets as a consequence. However, such errors are not numerous; so no undue worry need be experienced.

### IV. Pristella

There is probably no "most popular" fish in this group, for many of the family, being long in demand as aquarium stock, have established themselves in favor during the various stages of feverish excitement on the part of the aquarists, and have settled down into the position of reliable standbys, well accustomed and conditioned to the vicissitudes of domestic aquaria.

It is worth noting that many of the species of this family are fairly translucent, showing their backbones without much reticence, but none of them reaches the obviousness of the glass fish of India, which is so transparent as to be almost invisible in parts of his body. Despite this, however, a great diversity of color and pattern is visible in various species of the Characins.

An example is Pristella—*Pristella riddlei* is the correct name —but the fish is so well known that he needs no common name other than the shortened one. This fellow is less than two inches long when full grown and exhibits a fairly good X-ray of himself against the light. He comes from the Amazon and points north, as far as Venezuela, and is quite attractively marked. He is shiny-looking, and has a black spot just behind and above the gill covers, and another on both the anal and dorsal fins. Both of these latter are bordered by a yellow and a white mark. The tail is red. The sexes may be distinguished by the very much heavier body of the female, and by the shape of the ovaries, which are round at the ends, and visible when the fish is held against the light. The male organs are pointed.

## V. Hemigrammus and Hyphessobrycon

A somewhat similar fish from much the same regions is the One-lined Characin, *Hemigrammus unilineatus*. This fish is not so glassy and has no red fins. There is a somewhat similar pattern on the dorsal and anal fins, however, but the yellow color, and sometimes the shoulder spot, is missing. The general color effect is silver, with a widening dark line starting about the middle of the body and expanding toward the tail, the base of which it covers.

A fish similar to the last, but with a distinctly reddish tinge over most of the body, deepening as it nears the tail, is the Rosy Characin, *Hyphessobrycon rosaceus*. It comes from the Amazon only. The fins share the general redness of the body, but the dorsal and anal fins are marked with bright orange and across them runs a distinct black line. This fish also has a shoulder spot.

The Flame Characin, *Hyphessobrycon flammeus,* from Rio de Janeiro, resembles *Hyphessobrycon rosaceus* in size—about one and a half inches long—and in general coloration. He is, however, a little deeper in the body, across which, between the gills and the dorsal fin, run three bars. The first ray of the dorsal is pale, probably green or yellow in color, or perhaps white, depending on the light in which one sees it. In the male this coloration is duplicated on the anal fin, which, together with the ventral fins, is edged with black. The red of the body of this fish is more brilliant than in *Hyphessobrycon rosaceus* and is slightly orange in hue. The usual name given this animal in aquatic circles is Red Tetra, a name which has been his since he was first introduced into America as *Tetragonopterus.* It is always a good plan, though, to learn the correct scientific names of fishes, for confusion frequently attends attempts to convey information about a fish passing under a nickname in one locality which name may be completely unknown in another or, worse, which may be used for a different fish there.

A fish of which its owner always speaks with a certain amount of pride is *Hemigrammus ulreyi,* Ulrey's Characin, of the Paraguay region. This little fellow, about one and a half inches long, is another of the silver or silvery-green translucent fishes. Though of the same general shape as *Pristella riddlei,* he has much more color in his make-up. Through the body, there is a series of lines which appear to be red, white and blue, but these lines are so close together, and change so subtly as the fish moves, that they are not always easy to distinguish. However, a spot on the shoulder, another on the dorsal fin, a black stripe on the base of the anal fin, delicately colored with pink, and a pinkish tail, complete the color scheme.

For some reason not clear, these Ulreys do not seem to thrive in aquaria, although if they are ever established, they live for a great while and grow heavy and sedate. Just why they should be so delicate and susceptible to changes of one sort or other when fish of many related species from the same localities thrive is one of those mysteries the aquarist becomes familiar with, without being able to solve. If a few of these fishes are established in a community aquarium and not bothered, they take a firm grip on life and seem to wax so fat on the artificial foods that persons who know them well in the state in which they come to us look twice and even three times to make sure they are Ulreys. These fishes are reported as breeding in a slightly different manner from most of their relatives. The eggs are liberated singly, and are eaten almost immediately in those rare cases when breeding in tanks has occurred, but since it is all but impossible to distinguish sex, I imagine we shall not be able to purchase breeding pairs for some time.

There is a fish of similar appearance fairly common in aquaria. This is the Striped Characin, *Hyphessobrycon heterorhabdus*, from the Lower Amazon. The difference between this species and the Ulreys is that the latter has scales on its tail— a purely technical difference which need not bother the aquarist, who probably would not be able to distinguish between living specimens anyway. After all, most aquarists are looking for lovely fishes which can be kept alive for a reasonable time in their tanks, and the name under which beauty appears is more or less immaterial. This species, and the Ulrey proper are both known to the aquarists as Ulreys.

Another Characin of about the same length does not offer nearly as much difficulty. This, the Head and Tail Light, is known as *Hemigrammus ocellifer* and comes from the Amazon. His curious popular name is derived from the red eye with the distinct shoulder spot behind it and the oddly colored spot at the base of the tail. This is really four spots grouped about a fine gold or black cross. The upper of the spots is red, and the whole effect is that of a reddish light shining through a golden haze. It is very attractive. This fish also is a translucent green in body color, with a slightly orange-yellow tinge in the ventral, dorsal and anal fins. The two latter are tipped with black, and both sexes are alike. The dorsal of the male, however, is slightly pointed.

The hatching of the eggs of this species takes about twice as long as the average for the group. The young are free of the eggs five days after they are liberated. There are, of course, variations in the period of incubation in this as in all other animals, but five days is about the average.

None of these fishes is particularly active. Their usual attitude is one in which they seem suspended from the surface of the water, and if there are a number of any species in an aquarium, they usually "school" together, and swim in the same direction. For long periods, the total activity of such a school will be nothing more than a few quick jerks with the pectoral fins, which seem to unfold, flash rapidly and fold up or become invisible again.

There is a fish similar to the Red Tetra, but yellow in color. As might be supposed, this is called the Yellow Tetra, although his name is *Hyphessobrycon bifasciatus*. This is a native of Southeastern Brazil, and is quite popular in North America. It is about two inches long when full grown, and in its youth it carries a red spot on dorsal, anal and tail fins. This disappears with age. The sexes are differentiated by fine distinctions. These include the longer ventral fins, the round, red-bordered anal fin, and the white tip at the front and top of the dorsal fin of the male. The female lacks these.

The name "Guppy" is by far the best known in tropical fish circles. The fish we know by that name is the miniature *Lebistes reticulatus*, previously mentioned. This fellow carries the name "Guppy" solely by usage. There is a Characin, however, not very well known, which bears the designation officially. *Hemibrycon guppyi* comes from Trinidad whenever he gets here at all. These fishes are about three and a half inches long, and deposit many eggs at a time. As many as six or eight hundred are reported.

So few of these fish ever come in that there is no danger of confusion arising from the similarity of names.

## VI. Astyanax

*Astyanax bimaculatus* is a fairly common fish in American aquaria, but is not held in much esteem because it is not particularly bright in color. It is, however, quite as lively and handsome as many others, and should not be overlooked if a tankful of Characins is being built up. It has a somewhat distressful habit of chewing plants, but for some reason does not bother the Dwarf Sagittaria. As its name indicates, it has two spots, one on the shoulder, and the other at the base of of the tail. Its name does not indicate the bright red dorsal, anal and tail fins—the brightest parts of the fish. Under excellent conditions, the fish grows to about six inches, but it is hardly ever brought in that size and seldom reaches it in tanks. It lives in a variety of waters, which in some cases may be brackish, and in others may be quite cold, for its range reaches from nearly tide water in the streams of Northeastern South America to streams high in the mountains. There are no sex marks.

The Banded Astyanax, *Astyanax fasciatus,* is quite a small fellow, about three inches long, but he is quite a nuisance to the bathers of his haunts, for he attacks in large numbers persons who venture into his streams. Examination of the contents of the stomachs of many specimens indicate that he is an indefatigable scavenger, always a welcome addition to the aquarium.

The range of this fish is very wide. Specimens are taken on both sides of Central America as far north as Mexico, and along the eastern seaboard to Buenos Aires. There are no recorded differences between the sexes, but the experienced eye may catch small indications in the general shape of the animal.

A Characin from the United States is increasing in popularity. This is not particularly good-looking although it has a blue line running the length of the body from head to tail, and a spot on the tail. It is called *Astyanax mexicanus,* for it is generally taken in Mexico. The range, however, extends north of the Rio Grande in the streams feeding that river. Full-grown specimens do not exceed four inches in length.

## VII. "Spilurus"

A fish of whose welcome in aquaria there seems to be some uncertainty is *Ctenobrycon spilurus,* for periodically, there is a revival of interest in it, followed by a period when it is never even mentioned. This fish is usually known as Spilurus, and is an excellent example of a phenomenon fairly common among fish. This is the tiny hooks on the anal fin which have to do with breeding. These hooks are usually too small to be seen, but may be recognized by the fingers if the tips are gently rubbed along the fin. The method of distinguishing sexes of fish by netting several and letting them fall back into the water, marking those that fall first as females and the last as males, has been specifically used for years with this fish. The hooks of the fin stick momentarily in the material of the net, thus holding the fish longer than one that has no hooks. This fish is slightly different from any of the Characins mentioned so far. It is rather deep in the body, and roughly resembles the conventional diamond shape, with the corners rounded. On a silvery body the fish sports a short green lateral line, starting about half way between the head and tail, as well as a dark spot on the tail. The male is smaller than the female, which may be three inches long, and lacks the red tint present on the anal fin of the female. This is an Amazon River fish.

## VIII. Red-finned Characin

A really bright little fish about two inches long is the Red-finned Characin. This, *Aphyocharax rubripinnis,* is an Argentinian, living principally in the vicinity of Rosario. It has the regular fish-shaped body, and also has anal hooks in the male. The color is silver, but the fins are a livid blood-red—quite startlingly so. The eggs of this species are different from the general run of Characin in that they are not adhesive. They follow the general rule of incubation, hatching within two days.

## IX. Fresh-water Flying Fishes

The fishes which have caused the greatest stir in recent years are the fresh-water flying fish. There are several genera of these, but only two species are in any way popular. The others are almost never imported, although they are all found in the same general region of the Amazon, near its mouth, and some of them as far north as Panama.

All these fishes show a very peculiar shape, somewhat reminiscent of the head of an ax, which has caused them all to be known by the rather appropriate name of Hatchetfish. The lower profile of the body is very convex, while the upper is very slightly convex, almost straight, in fact. This tremendous development of the chest is solely due to the development of the muscles attached to the pectoral fins, which are quite large and which are used as "wings" when the fish leaves the water. This they do in schools, leaping out and flying a few inches above the surface for six or eight feet, a long way when we consider that a fish two and a half or three inches long is quite large. There is no way to distinguish sex, as far as we know, and the fish never has been reported to fly out of an aquarium. Nor has it been reported as breeding, so we are dependent on imported stock for our specimens.

There are two different kinds of Hatchetfish commonly imported. They are easily distinguished. One, *Gasteropelicus sternicla* is a silvery-green all over, while the other, *Carnegiella strigata,* is mottled with irregular slanting lines of brown, nearly black. A third Hatchetfish. *Thoracocharax securis,* is similar to *Gasteropelicus sternicla* in color and shape, but the lower edge of the body over the anal fin is black. *Thoracocharax maculatus,* the largest, is three inches long and has the same general pattern as *Gasteropelicus sternicla,* but also carries a few black marks along its sides.

These fishes are particularly fond of small aquatic insects. They probably live entirely upon such food in the wild state. Care must be exercised to see that they are taking dried food, if that is offered them, for they have to be more or less trained to each such stuff. If they are placed in an aquarium with other fish which eat the foods offered, and the food is one of the slow-sinking kind, the flying fish will soon learn. Otherwise, they may starve themselves to death before they discover that the food offered is edible.

## X. South American Glass Fish

Occasionally a fish with a curious "dish face" appears. There are one or two species of the genus possessing such a characteristic continually bobbing up. Because the young of these species are more or less translucent, they are all generally known as the South American Glass Fish. The dorsal profile of the head is very concave, giving to the genus the name Rœboides. None of these ever brought into North America has been over four inches long, and they are all equally colorless and uninteresting-looking fishes, but for the man who likes novelty, here is one— or two, if he can get two species.

The range of the genus extends from the Amazon as far north and west as Colombia, and all of the fishes are a greenish-silver or yellow, with a few black spots of small size scattered about over the body. There does not seem to be any distinctive mark on the sexes, and no one knows anything of the spawning behavior. On the other hand, they are so seldom imported, and in such little demand, that no one appears to want to know anything of the spawning. They are all fairly quick at snapping up young Guppies, or other fish of a like smallness, and do not hesitate to tackle fishes somewhat bigger than babies. They are, however, peaceful if they are kept with fish their own size, and are not afflicted with any planticidal phobias.

## XI. The "Head-standing Fishes"

A fish with a remarkable color scheme is a relative of all these Characins. He comes from the northeastern shoulder of South America, and looks as if he were painted by a man with a jaundiced eye. Over a lemon-yellow body there are five jet black lines. These run around the animal. That, in itself, is not so bad, but as he grows in years—months, perhaps, would be a better measure of the age of a fish—the bands start splitting. First the first band splits into two separate bands, each half of which grows away from the other; then the next one splits, and so on down the length of the body until the fully mature fish has ten or twelve of these rings, resembling the stripes of a convict uniform. Then, as if all that color were not enough, the supports of the fins are all of different colors. The rays of the dorsal fin are blue; those of the tail fin darker—almost black; the pectoral rays are pink, and the anal fin rays are orange. The rays of the ventral fins are a dull brownish and red. The membrane covering the fin rays is more or less transparent, but it dulls somewhat the effect of all these colors unless the fish is observed in a very good light. In any case, as the fish grows older, the colors fade. The black rings almost disappear; the bright yellow turns into a brassiness.

This fish, *Leporinus fasciatus,* is one of the species called by old-time German aquarists the "Head-standing Fishes," because of their proclivity for staying more or less motionless with their heads near the bottom of the water and their tails up. If an ordinary fish should lie like this for any length of time, it would get into much the same difficulty we would if we stood on our heads for more than a minute or two. But these fishes seem to suffer no inconvenience whatever.

Another fish which likes to balance itself tail up is *Chilodus punctatus*. This, a high-backed, thin fish, is colored a sort of silver with a brownish tone, and has a black line, sometimes broken into spots, along its side from mouth to tail. It is not at all good-looking or pretty, but is quite suitable as a filler in an aquarium full of more spectacular fishes. It is about three and a half inches long, when it is full grown.

## XII. The Copeinas

There is a little fish whose habits entitle it to entrée into the most conservative aquarium. This is *Copeina arnoldi,* long and favorably known by the name of *Pyrrhulina filamentosa,* or just Filamentosa. This fish, believe it or not, lays its eggs out of water, hopping up several inches above the surface for this purpose, and then, just to make its queerness complete, spends the next two days or so splashing water up to keep the eggs wet! At least the male does. The female does not seem to care whether the eggs are wet or not. However, she is not to blame, for she has not the englarged fins the male has; so she cannot splash a great deal even if she wishes to.

Just why any fish should ever have invented such unusual behavior, or inherited so remarkable an instinct, is not at all clear, but it is a fact that the pair of fishes, after selecting a suitable rock or leaf, spring out of the water together, cling to the surface for a few seconds and then drop back into the water, leaving the eggs attached to whatever it was they selected. Then for the next two or two and a half days, the male splashes water over the eggs three or four times every hour. If the spawning is not completed at one time, several sites may be chosen for the eggs, and then the male, either remembering where they are, or sufficiently clear sighted to see them, chases around splashing water on them all in turn. The young when hatched are washed down into the water, and there is no record of any further parental care. It is quite possible that one or the other of the parents eats all the youngsters it can find.

There is another peculiarity about *Copeina arnoldi*. The males are distinctly larger than the females, a thing unheard of in orthodox fish society. The dorsal fin and the upper half of the tail fin are much larger in the male than in the female, and it is by means of these enlarged fins that the fish splashes up the water. Neither sex is spectacularly colored. Both are a sort of dusty brown, with a touch of red or yellow on the dorsal fin and a spot of red on the caudal fin. There are black edges on the scales, which give the fish a speckled effect, but the black is in very fine lines, and is not easily noticed. This fellow comes from the Amazon region. The males are about three inches long—half an inch less for the females.

A fish of the same genus is *Copeina guttata.* This one is a little larger than his relative, and a little more brightly colored. Each scale has a red dot which, in some lights, gives the fish an appearance of being lined with violet. The colors are more intense in the male, as is to be expected, and much more in evidence during the breeding period. This, while not nearly so strange as *Copeina arnoldi,* is still sufficiently unusual for a Characin to be worth mentioning. The eggs, often deposited in concentric circles on the flat, cleaned surface of a stone, are continually picked over and washed off with a stream of water created by the male by wiggling his fins above them. This goes on for two days or so, sometimes longer, and there are many more eggs than in the case of *Copeina arnoldi,* which usually has fewer than a hundred. There may be as many as a thousand deposited on the stone. This larger number may or may not be due to the larger size of the fish, sometimes four inches long. As with so many of the Characins, this fish makes its home in the Amazon.

## XIII. The Kite Fish

When we have discussed the Kite Fish, we are going to leave the Characins. This fish, with an impressive scientific name, *Pseudocorynopoma doriæ,* comes from South Brazil and Uruguay, and is only about three inches when it is full grown. The male has, however, a terrifically enlarged dorsal fin which is usually carried folded along the back. This probably has something to do with the courting gestures,—intricate and entertaining little dances apparently quite effective in wooing the female. This fish scatters its eggs about plants and does not pay them any further attention. The colors of the fish are, starting from top to bottom, brownish green; a fairly bright line from the head to a spot at the tail, and silvery. There are two spots on the tail fin, one at either extremity of the lobes and often a similar one on the pectoral. The whole fish seems covered with a metallic sheen. It is not particularly beautiful, but is in fair demand whenever it does arrive in the local stores.

The few African species of this family are comparatively unknown, so we will not bother with them.

# Chapter 8

## The Cichlids

THE NEXT family on the list, with the exception of one or two of its members, are all fighting fishes with bad tempers. These are spread fairly evenly over the tropic zones of America and Africa, with a few representatives south of the Tropic of Capricorn and a few more north of the Tropic of Cancer in America. They are usually solitary beasts, moping about in a little kingdom which they set up for themselves, and establishing very strict immigration laws. For smaller fish, any infringement of these laws is death, and larger fishes have to offer considerable and persistent resistance to ouster proceedings initiated against them. However, since the various species persist, there must be some relaxation of these regulations, else the females and males would never get together long enough to produce any families.

Almost all of these fishes have a very definitely developed nursery scheme, for they take meticulous care of their young for quite a long period. Sometimes this time is as long as six or eight weeks, and if any fish thinks he has found a Tartar when he barges into the area set apart by one of these fishes, he will think he has found a whole tribe of Tartars when he wanders into the vicinity of a growing family of Cichlids. (The name of the family we are speaking of is the Cichlidæ.)

The outstanding exception to this general unsociability is the Scalare, which is usually a perfectly peaceful fish. But there are all sorts of gradations in behavior, although they all have to do with the reproduction of young. A good many of these Cichlids will not bother one of the opposite sex, although care must be exercised at all times, for a pair of fishes, living in connubial bliss may at any moment turn the aquarium into an arena in which each struggles to destroy the other.

84

## I. Parental Care

A curious development of the breeding of these fishes is parental care. A paragraph or so ago, I said that the youngsters are under the guardianship of their parents for a long period, but I did not say that the male is usually the most active in this rôle. Indeed, he is sometimes the only guardian the babies have, for if he does not drive the female away, she wanders off of her own accord. However, it is quite a frequent sight to see one of the parents shepherding the flock of tiny fishes about their home while the other does a sort of outpost duty, driving off any fishes before they are within a foot or two of the other parent and their fry. When a pair of fishes assume these rôles, they usually take turns in the immediate or distant defense of their offspring, and it is rather wonderful to watch how one will come into the group and the other immediately sail off on the scouting detail. This is particularly noticeable if a pair of Cichlids are nursing a swarm of small fishes in a large tank in which there are other fishes. If the feeding of the inhabitants of the aquarium takes place at a definite corner of the tank, the babies will be held in a group at a far corner, with one parent in close attendance, while the other holds the other fishes near the feeding corner. When the food is offered, the fish nearest will take a few hasty mouthfuls, and then dash off to relieve the other, who without hesitation, swims over to dine, keeping a wary eye on the strange fish all the while. Such behavior as this is particularly noticeable in the genus *AEquidens,* a few species of which are always available, but not always welcome.

Still more remarkable is the behavior of many of the African Cichlids. As far as we know, all the species of two genera of this family subscribe to this habit, but in such an uncertain world it is never safe to say "all" or "each," especially when talking of fishes, for apparently as soon as one makes a definite statement that thus and so is the case, something heretofore unheard of will turn up to spoil the statement. Still, as far as we know, all the Tilapias and Haplochromis, instead of making holes into which the eggs are deposited as is the habit of the Cichlids of our side of the world, make the hole, deposit the eggs, and then pick them up and store them in one or the other of the parents' mouths until they hatch. This may take three weeks, but the fish still carries them, getting thinner and more comet-like in appearance all the while, for during the time the eggs are being incubated, the fish does not eat and becomes very attenuated. Some of the fishes even carry the young for a few days or a week after they are hatched, releasing them for short periods, but opening their mouths to receive them back again at the first sign of a disturbance. In this latter case, the unfortunate parent grows more and more like a tadpole, for as the body becomes thinner, the mouth parts expand to accommodate the growing youngsters within.

## II. Tilapias and Their Relatives

All of the imported Tilapias to date are mouthbreeders. There are one or two from the west coast of Africa, closely related and similar in appearance. *Tilapia heudeloti* occurs in that part of West Africa which faces south, and *Tilapia dolloi* from just south of that region, where the coastline changes and faces west. It also occurs inland, as far east as the Upper Congo. The first is half as long again as the second, but since aquarium specimens are seldom seen exceeding four or five inches, instead of the twelve and eight inches respectively of the *heudeloti* and *dolloi* in freedom, we need not stress the point.

Both of these fishes are a pale gray, with bold black splotches about the head and under the chin. In both species it is apparently a matter of indifference which of the parents picks up and carries the eggs, for both sexes have been observed in this unusual solicitude. When these fishes first appeared on the American scene, a year or two ago, there was somewhat of a scramble on the part of aquarists to procure some of them, but since it was discovered that they bred on the slightest provocation, and fought on none, they have lost caste, and it is frequently impossible to give them away! Neither of them is particularly pugnacious in aquaria, but they will, on occasion, pick at other fishes.

Of similar habits, but a little larger, is another Tilapia from the east coast of Africa as far south as Natal. This is *Tilapia natalensis,* not greatly different in appearance from its relatives from the west. The females of all these species of fishes are not so well marked as the males, but otherwise are not noticeably different.

During the time of incubation, and immediately after it, the moving shadows of the young fish may be observed through the translucent opercular covering at the side of the head of the parent carrying them. This causes considerable excitement in the breasts of the fond aquarists experiencing the thrill of breeding these fishes for the first time, and is worthy of note by more blasé individuals.

The actual courtship of these animals preparatory to mating is not in the least suggestive of more usual love-making. Both fishes face each other, mouth agape in the most threatening manner. A few inches separate them; and as one advances, the other retreats, keeping the same distance apart. The movements are stiff and jerky, as if both were models of fishes suspended from a series of strings like marionettes. After a moment or two of such maneuvers, one breaks away, and both swim casually about the tanks as if there were nothing more important on their minds than finding an odd bit of food. Then suddenly they are both facing each other again, and the whole business is resumed. After a period of such goings-on, the eggs are deposited in a hole in the dirt or sand or pebbles of the floor of the aquarium, which has been previously prepared by one or both of the fish.

Of about the same size, eighteen inches long, is another Tilapia, *Tilapia nilotica,* from a large area extending from the Upper Congo region of Africa to the small but famous Lake Galilee in Palestine. On the strength of this fish's coming from the waters of Palestine, in Asia, I suppose it would be logical to say that Cichlids come from Asia as well as from America and Africa, but so few ever do come in that the average aquarist's idea that all the aquarium Cichlids are either of American or African origin is substantially correct. There is a Tilapia, *zilli,* of that ilk, which is reported to have a range identical with that of *nilotica,* and to be of very similar appearance, but which is not supposed to be a "mouth-breeder," as such fishes are called. This may be so, but there are so few of these fishes captured and transported to aquaria where their general life history may be observed that it is not possible to say whether both names cover the same fish, or whether neither or both or only the first, if they are different fishes, has adopted the peculiarities usual for the genus. However that may be, there is no question about the breeding habits of the genus *Haplochromis*, of which the only two species known are old acquaintances of the aquarists. The first, the Egyptian Mouthbreeder, *Haplochromis strigigena* has a range extending from the mouth of the Nile right on down through Uganda to Tanganyika Territory. It is probably to be found in Ethiopia on the one side of that range, and along the eastern edge of the Belgian Congo on the west. (It is advisable to have an atlas of the world at hand when tracing the locales of these various fishes, for, like postage stamps, they come from places no one but the expert geographer can place.) But since no one has found them outside of the Nile Valley and regions beyond that river's headwaters, we must not wander far afield in our statements that a fish comes from this and not that place.

This Egyptian fish is a little fellow, hardly ever reaching a length of three inches, and is quite brightly colored in metallic shades of green, gold and blue. The fins of the male are similarly decorated, with an even greater variety of tints, including yellow and black. The female, generally lighter, has hardly any color on her fins at all. At times, both the fishes grow considerably paler, showing no more than a yellowish gray over most of the body. This is *not* at breeding time, when both sexes put on their best and most colorful livery. These fishes will carry the eggs and young for about two weeks, and while the female usually assumes the unpleasant task of starving while her mouth is full (of eggs and young), the male will sometimes be chivalrous and take over the nursery duty.

The other *Haplochromis*, specifically *moffati*, comes from the Congo headwaters, and is about half as big again as its Egyptian relative. It has the same general habits, but is not nearly so colorful. Its general service uniform is dark olive, with a sprinkling of dull red gold and blue dots, one on each scale. The male has the added distinction of a bright mark at the extremity of the anal fin. Besides fading in color at times, both these fishes seem able to change the pattern to some small degree, showing bars across the body at one time, and none at others.

One or two formerly very popular Cichlids originate in Africa. These do not use their buccal cavities as nurseries, but incubate the eggs either in depressions dug in the sand at the bottom of the aquarium or on flat stones to which they are attached. In any case, after the fry are wrigglers, but before they can swim about under their own power, they are transferred more or less continually by one or the other parent to other holes and depressions. Whether or not this is done because the food supply in the immediate neighborhood of the nest runs out or for sanitary reasons we do not know, but it is more or less characteristic of all the Cichlids. The fishes in question are popularly known as "Jewelfish," the one called "Ruby" being the best known. This is a red fish, over which is liberally spread a collection of emerald and sapphire-like spots. The male is much more highly colored than the female, and at the mating season he puts on such a show that he looks quite black. At this time, both sexes are particularly savage, retreating from their stone with its load of eggs only in the most dire extremity. Even the comparatively huge hand of a man will not drive them away, but will suffer a few deep enough bites to make it withdraw instead! This fish, also known as the Red Chromide, and scientifically as *Hemichromis bimaculatus,* comes from 'way inland in Africa, where the Nile and Congo Rivers spend their youth.

Another Jewelfish, *Hemichromis fasciatus,* comes from nearer the seacoast to the west, down Angola way. This has never found favor because of its bad habits. This fish would never have made a Horatio Alger hero, for he fights with everything. He also tears up plants, digs holes all over the place, and, finally, grows too big for the ordinary aquarium. A full-grown Banded Jewelfish is ten inches long, and would attempt to lick his weight in wildcats. His habits, as far as they are known, are similar to his smaller but not less fierce relative. However, the smaller size of the first makes him seem less savage, just as a really savage mosquito would not look as dangerous as a comparatively tame bull. Apart from all this, the fish is not particularly brightly colored, so there is no real reason why he should ever be kept as a pet.

One or two species of the genus *Pelmatochromis*—*arnoldi* and *subocellatus*—come from the coastal area of the Gulf of Guinea. These are a little more peaceful. They are also a little more conservative in costume, and only about one-third to one-half as long as the Banded Jewelfish. They have never been very popular, although this may be due to their comparative scarceness. However, if we take into consideration the fact that both of them are really quite nice-looking fish which breed fairly readily in captivity, and that they will not interfere with other fishes of a comparable size, we will have to confess that we do not know why so few are available, for many other fishes not nearly so suited to domestic aquaria are to be obtained at all times. As with the other Cichlids, the distinction between the sexes is that the males have the brightest or greatest variety of color, and the spawning habits are similar to the Jewelfish.

## III. Scalare

We leave the Africanders here and go to the more generally known Americans. As we said before, these are spread out over all of tropical and sub-tropical America, and send more representatives for their lesser numbers to our aquaria than their relations in the Old World. However, while all the breeding behavior is interesting, it is not so spectacular as that of the Mouth-breeders, and the colors, while high in many cases, are not so high or handsome as the Jewelfish. Proximity, or the greater number of ships between North America and their homes, must be the cause of their greater popularity, for it cannot be their behavior, which, in a good many cases, is just as offensive as is that of the Banded Jewelfish.

The gentle, sedate Scalare, frequently called the Angelfish, is a Brazilian Cichlid. This is an exceptionally well-behaved member of the family, for, excluding a few unconsidered young Guppies which he relishes and considers a highly desirable food, he will not bother any fishes he may find quartered in his tank. Once in a while a bad-tempered old fish of either sex may turn up, but in general the behavior is exemplary.

Until the last year or so, this fish was the most highly prized of aquarium fishes, bringing prices as high as thirty and forty dollars a pair for good specimens. But since there is no definite way of distinguishing sex externally, it has always been a matter of conjecture as to whether there was a pair or only two of a kind. However, acute aquarists have discovered that such fishes may breed in suitable aquaria, and so the price has fallen until it has to be a very exceptional pair to bring even six or eight dollars now. Young fish are sold at less than a dollar each, a terrific slight to the King of the Aquarium, as he is often called.

The dorsal and anal fins of this silver and black beauty are extended so greatly above and below the general body line that the fish actually measures more from top to bottom than from start to finish. *Pterophyllum scalare*, full grown, is reputed to reach about six inches in length, but aquarium specimens seldom attain such a size, and fishes about half as long are considered large.

The black lines, of which there are four across the body, as well as the very compressed shape, would suggest that the fish is an inhabitant of reedy waters, and the method of reproduction would confirm this, for the eggs are deposited on the stiff stalks of plants, to which they adhere, instead of being placed in nest-like depressions or on stones which is so common a practice among the Cichlids. These characteristics, together with the almost total absence of combativeness, and tolerance of plants about it, are really remarkable when we consider the general practice of all its near relatives. Then, too, the shape of the fish is strikingly different, with its circular body and elongated fins, looking like the points of a crescent moon.

This fish attaches its eggs to the stiff stalks of plants in rows, and has been fooled by many aquarists into putting them on glass rods which may be removed without much disturbance and placed in rearing tanks, similar to any other except that they are usually shallow and are free of large fishes which would enjoy a breakfast of fresh eggs.

It was the discovery of the fact that these fish breed in a slightly acid type of water that caused the sudden storm about pH among aquarium-minded persons. From the appearance of the fish, however, such a preference is to be expected, for a fish so thin from side to side and with such a color scheme would probably live in fairly stagnant water with plenty of reedy stalks to hide in. In such waters there is always a mass of decaying vegetation, and the colors of the fish suggest a quantity of shading plants at the surface which would retard the photosynthesis of plants, thereby causing an accumulation of carbon dioxide to be built up to lower the pH of the water until it is acid.

Semi-scientific literature lists other fishes of the same general build as the Scalare, giving them specific names, but the differences are so small that it is very uncertain whether or not there is more than one species, although there may be several races from slightly different environments. Taxonomists, who specialize in describing minute differences between one fish and another, when the differences are standard and unvarying, do not indicate definitely that there is any other species, so I do not think we should become exercised about it.

There is a fish of the same general body outline, but without the same large fin spread, which comes from pretty much the same area. It, however, has more black lines on the sides— about twice as many—is of a brownish-green body color with blue along the margin and has a different dentition. This fish is called the Blue Scalare, *Symphysodon discus* and is quite expensive whenever it arrives from the Amazon. A recent shipment brought from $50 to $100 a fish. It is about seven or eight inches long and very reticent about its breeding habits, never having demonstrated them to even the most persistent investigators. However, since it is taken in much the same waters as the Scalare, and is of much the same build, it might be in order to assume that it has much the same proclivities, although the careful scientist assumes nothing, for the very good reason that things which should follow from the facts at hand are usually upset and do not follow because there are other facts, just as pertinent, not at hand. However, these same persistent inquirers never tire in their search for the hidden mysteries; so I have no doubt that somewhere, sometime, someone will announce with pride that a pair of these Disc Cichlids, as they may justly be called, has spawned in one of his tanks. We will know all about it then, although we may not be able to duplicate his announcement by having a pair spawn in our tank.

## IV. Cichlasoma

A fish of an entirely different character has recently achieved some small popularity. This is quite an old acquaintance, but until a discerning aquarist called it "Jack Dempsey," in honor of its excellent pugilistic qualities, it was inclined to be overlooked by people seeking fishes to stock their aquaria. Since then it has received a measure of public recognition quite well justified by its good looks and interesting habits. As with most fishes, these are particularly concerned with the rearing of a family.

First, a stone is selected which has a rather large flat surface. This is thoroughly scoured with sand and small pebbles which the fish sprays from its mouth—both sexes spend many hours in this preparation. After a final polishing done by mouth, the female deposits the eggs in a more or less continuous ribbon around and around a central spot. Sometimes there are more than the surface of the stone will accommodate, so the edges are covered too. The male follows all the movements of the female closely, fertilizing the eggs. For the next few days, neither fish strays far from the eggs, but hovers about them, continually picking off bits of matter which may settle in their vicinity. It is also assumed that they pick off eggs which may not be developing; not at all too rash an assumption, for there certainly appear spaces in the string of eggs after the first day or two.

After a period of about four days, or perhaps six, the fry will be free of the eggs. Then they are watched very closely by both parents, who continually move them from one depression to another in the sandy or pebbly bottom. The young cannot swim freely for several days; but after they start swimming, they are kept in a close group, both parent fish taking part in all the manœuvers. If one infant strays away, it is immediately seized in the mouth of its father or mother and brought back, and the whole family is kept in constant motion from one place to another in a more or less circumscribed area. At this time, the parent fish will attack the hand of any person foolish enough to put it in the water, and a sizable bite will be the penalty. Fry may be tended by the parents until they are half an inch long, but they are usually free to follow their own devices before they are quite so big. They then speedily learn that the erstwhile protecting jaws of their parents are good things to stay away from, for the babies are appreciated as tasty morsels after they have been driven from home. These fish are formally called *Cichlasoma nigrofasciatum*, and their care of the young is duplicated by many of their close relatives. So, too, is their pugnacity and dislike of strange fish. Full-sized specimens are about eight inches long, but they are infrequently encountered as large as that in North America. They originate in Guatemala.

## V. The Acaras

A fish which, with the exception of the original stone, acts similarly about its offspring is the Blue Acara. This, officially *AEquidens latifrons*, usually places its eggs in depressions it digs for their reception at the outset, although it will sometimes use a stone or even the glass of the aquarium, but the afterhatching activity is almost identical. Several pairs of these fish have spawned at the same time in opposite corners of a large aquarium. The wanderings of the various broods seemed to threaten complications, for the paths of the groups frequently overlapped and the broods met occasionally. There was not, however, any fighting between the guardians of the respective broods, which seemed to sort themselves out very nicely. At least, every pair of fish seemed to have the same number of youngsters it had before; but whether it lost some of its own babies and adopted some of the other pair's, it is impossible to say. With such highly organized behavior, it would not be unreasonable to suppose that each fish got all of its own babies, which may have sufficient identifying insignia for the parent to recognize, or they may carry a sort of group smell. *AEquidens latifrons* inhabits the streams and rivers of the northernmost countries of South America, from Panama to Venezuela. It is quite a bright fish, with a blue spot in each scale and fins shaded with green and bordered, in the case of the dorsal, with brilliant brick red. The tail fin is reddish instead of green. Aquarium specimens are usually three or four inches long, and while it is not especially bad-tempered, it is not to be trusted with other, smaller fish, or even with fish of a comparative size, for it can, and will, render a very good account of itself in a free-for-all.

Another AEquidens from Southern Brazil, northward and westward through Paraguay to Bolivia, is a little smaller, and because it is of a bluish tint, is often confused with the Blue Acara. This is *AEquidens portalegrensis*, named for the romantic-sounding Port Alegre. The scientific names of fishes usually mean something, and are quite descriptive; if one will take the trouble to translate them. For instance, *AEquidens latifrons* means the fish "with teeth of the same size and a broad forehead," while *AEquidens portalegrensis* means the fish "with teeth of the same size, from Port Alegre." The names are given by the ichthyologist who first describes the fish, the generic name—the first one—usually being related to some peculiarity, and the specific name—the second—either in honor of the person who caught it, or enabled it to be caught, or for the locality from which it came, or for some other peculiarity. Once in a while, the name may have no particular meaning, but is made up or has a fanciful bearing on a mark or the shape of the fish. The genus *Abudefduf* is so named because it has fat sides, and the name is composed of several Arabic words meaning the fish "having extra fat flanks."

*AEquidens portalegrensis* is quite a nice-looking fish, with just as interesting behavior as the other Cichlids, but is not a great favorite in domestic aquaria because it shares all the faults of the family. It will tear plants apart, fight and generally make itself a nuisance in a well-kept aquarium, thus rendering no assistance to the aquarist in his continual struggle to keep the algæ from obscuring the view.

There are a few more fishes of the genus *AEquidens* which are of the same general character as the two we have talked about, but they are in even less demand.

## VI. Chanchito

A fish with a very odd name in translation is the Chanchito. Its scientific name, *Cichlasoma facetum,* means "merry" or "good-humored," but the fish is not in any way sportive. Instead, it goes very seriously about its business of feeding and fighting whenever opportunity offers. This, too, is a handsome creature of a high golden color crossed with black bars, which may enlarge when the fish is courting until he is almost all black. An occasional specimen is encountered whose fins turn bright red at breeding time.

This fish, about eight inches long when it is full grown, attaches its eggs to stones or rocks and follows the usual Cichlidean custom of protecting its babies with the utmost vigor. He and she, for that matter, are very industrious at destroying plants, and since much of the plant disappears at the time of its destruction, some of it is probably eaten. This seems to be true of most of the family which may enjoy some green food once in a while. But they enjoy worms more, tackling and eating at one meal several worms longer than they are themselves. They also enjoy other fish if any are within reach, and will even eat snails, shells and all. In other words, they will eat almost anything.

## VII. Earth-eaters

The Chanchitos have not, however, quite so omnivorous an appetite as their close relatives of the genus *Geophagus,* whose name means "earth-eater." This genus has probably received the appellation from its habit of nosing about in the earth at the bottom of the water when it is building nests, for apart from some very small and very technical internal differences of structure, some of its species are identical with species of the genus *AEquidens,* especially in breeding habits. There are not many in the genus, and they are not particularly popular, but they are, in common with the other members of their family, quite handsome fishes.

These fishes have, in general, the same bad reputation as aquarium inhabitants, for they are efficient fighters when they choose to scrap, which is, when they are mature, fairly often.

Hoplias malabaricus

Lyretail

Chanchito spawning

Armored catfish

Sleeper

"Head-standing fish"

Knife fish

Corydoras

Leporinus

Siamese fighting fish

Jewelfish with eggs

Elongated cichlids fighting

Kissing gourami

Round-tailed fighting fish

Piranha

Crenuchus spilurus

There is one, however, which has been much maligned, whose name, "Demon Fish," is just about as misleading as it can be. The few specimens which have come under observation as aquarium fish have been much more peaceful than the most optimistic aquarist would expect any Cichlid to be. These may be exceptions, of course, but one would expect all the members of a species with such a name to be particularly unpleasant beasts. This unfortunately christened animal comes from an area between the Amazon River on the south and the Guianas on the north, and goes down in history as *Geophagus jurupari* —the Earth-eating Devilfish. What a name! But he doesn't know anything about it, so we need not worry for him. As we said before, all this group place their eggs, as do the AEquidens, in little depressions they dig in the sand for themselves, although they are not above taking advantage of any holes that may be available. The young are scrupulously tended and grow up into fishes about nine inches long, with large heads whose cheeks are spotted all over with blue. The spots run over onto the sides of the body, but aside from the blue, the fish is not very bright, a sort of indefiniteness between yellow and brown.

There is another little habit recorded of this fish which is worth mentioning, although few will have the opportunity to observe it, for the fish is almost never brought into North America. This habit has for its aim the protection of the grown fish, and is not usual with animals of a similar nature at all. The fish scouts about until it finds a flat rock, under which it tunnels, making an entrance at one side and an exit at the other. Into this hole it retreats when danger approaches. Record has it that the male does this, saying nothing about the female.

Whether she is sufficiently amazonic to defy danger, or whether the male is chivalrous enough to allow her to use his retreat, or whether the observations are faulty and miss the fact that the female also digs a passageway, we do not know. If this business of burrowing is true, it is noteworthy that the peaceful member of the family takes possession of its little kingdom and holds it by discretion rather than valor, as is the case with all its scrappy cousins.

The Red-finned Cichlid, a related fish, is much better-looking than this one, for its colors are much brighter. Probably for this reason, it is much more popular, although popularity is hardly the correct word to use, even in comparison, for the fish is quite unknown outside the circles of the most devoted aquarists. However, we shall compromise and say that the fish is in greater demand. This Red-finned Cichlid, *Geophagus brasiliensis,* is from the extreme northeastern part of Brazil. (The Amazon again, you notice.) As its name indicates, it has red fins, and is really quite a handsome fellow, for the body has a greenish sheen over a yellow base. As is usual, the colors deepen at maturity, especially when the fish are courting, which may occur at any time in domestic aquaria. These are not as destructive to plants as are their relatives, but they are not to be trusted in a really nicely planted aquarium, for they will dig holes in the sand at the bottom of the tank with little or no provocation, and the plants do not thrive in such a tank, even if they are not entirely torn apart. They are not to be trusted with other fishes, either, for they will fight with as much readiness as they will root about the tank, and their teeth are not to be despised as weapons in a fishy rough-and-tumble. The Red-finned Cichlids spawn on rocks, preferring a flat surface, and while a male and female thrown together by the exigencies of aquarium life may decide to become happy in mating, they may just as easily decide that they are incompatible. Divorce being unknown to them, they take the only course open and try to murder each other. For this reason, young specimens are more suitably mated, for they have not the intolerance of age, and are accustomed to each other's foibles by the time they are cranky enough to become destructive. It is just as well that they are not particularly prevalent in domestic aquaria.

There are one or two more Geophagus which are occasional visitors to our aquaria, but they are all pretty much the same as the last one, and much more infrequently seen, so we shall leave them in favor of more interesting fishes.

## VIII. The Chromides

"Indian Cichlid," "Orange Chromide" and *"Etroplus maculatus"* are all names of one little fish which is quite a peaceful Cichlid in every respect but that of the guardianship of the eggs and fry. Then it vigorously resents any interference of or approach to the nest with the utmost ferocity. Since it is quite small, though, this will not distrub any but the most cowardly of fishes; it is therefore best to leave a pair which have decided to reproduce their kind in an aquarium of their own. The Indian Cichlid is captured most frequently along the coast of Madras, India, where it is reported in both fresh and brackish waters. Specimens are also reported as coming from as far east as Burma and French Indo-China, but they are not apparently so authentically located as the Indian ones. Further reports from India make it clear that the fish is taken in large numbers for food, a horrible sacrilege in the eyes of the good aquarist. However, food or no food, the fish is a pretty little creature, about three inches long when caught wild, of a golden orange, with a suggestion of black along the back and in spots along the side. It has a curious habit of suspending its eggs from the roof of any cave-like structure it finds, using bits of wood or stone in nature, and readily substituting for these the inside of a flower-pot in the aquarium. After this preliminary, the typical digging of pits into which the young are carried may be observed, and the swarm of youngsters, after they are hatched, is escorted about the aquarium, and put to bed every night in small holes just as are the larger, more savage Cichlid babies. The hatching takes from five to ten days, and both parents are very careful of the nest and fry. Cases are recorded in which the parents quarrel considerably after the young are swimming about. It may be that neither one likes the way the other is educating the little fishes, and says so in no uncertain terms. During such altercations, any of the bones of contention may be accidentally snapped up, a distressing contretemps which may be avoided by taking the parent fish out of the nursery and letting them do their scrapping elsewhere.

Another Etroplus, *Etroplus suratensis,* from the Far East, resembles its relatives from South America, both in size—it is about twelve inches long—and habits, especially the undesirable ones of fighting and rip-snorting about the tank with unfortunate results to the aquatic vegetation. It is for this reason not considered very suitable for domestic aquaria.

# Chapter 9

## The Bubble-Nesters

THERE ARE a few more Cichlids scattered about between Burma and the upper reaches of the Amazon—about one hundred more—but most of them are not suitable for our purpose, and many of them are complete strangers to aquaria. So while we are over in Southeastern Asia we may as well have a look at a family of fishes with very remarkable habits, whose range centers about this locality.

This family is called Osphronemidæ, and most of its representatives are, within reason, good aquarium fishes. They are usually small animals, well adapted to life in the close confines of the aquarium, colorful and decorative and of particularly interesting habits. As usual with fishes, these are chiefly confined to propagation, for a fish seems to have nothing on its mind other than the preservation of its own body by eating and fighting, or the preservation of its kind by reproduction.

### I. Siamese Fighting Fish

There is a habit common to most of the species, however, which was perhaps originated in the desire to reproduce, and which finds its greatest manifestations at the breeding periods, without having anything whatever to do directly with the propagation of the species. This habit in one of the species has given rise to many legends about the Siamese Fighting Fish. It is reported upon very good authority that this fish, a native of Siam in particular and the Malay Peninsula in general, is used in encounters of a pugilistic nature, being bred for such purposes. However, there is no definite confirmation from competent observers that this is general, such reports as filter through the mass of travelers' fiction indicating that the sport is almost entirely confined to boys and very young men. Whatever the status of the business, that is, whether there are any breeding establishments for such fishes, or whether the animals are caught wild in their rice-field ditches and simply brought in to town to fight any other fish which may also have been brought in, the fish is undeniably pugnacious and willing to fight any other fish within reach. A considerable amount of paper has been covered with descriptions of the betting and excitement caused by such matches.

The males are the worst offenders against the peace, as may be supposed, and they will fight at any time, although they hold off their biting to indulge in a considerable amount of love play at appropriate moments. After their nests have been filled with eggs, however, the unfortunate female who was misled into a confiding trust by the dancing and posturing of the male, is driven off or killed, and the eggs are left to develop under the fiercely paternal care of the father. This is unceasing and remorseless, for the fish, which was a fighting fool before parenthood, develops into a veritable fury afterward, attacking anything that approaches the nest, never giving a thought to its own safety.

The eggs hatch in about two days after they have been spawned, and the young are kept in the nest for a few days longer, any that fall out of the nest being replaced immediately by the parent. After the young become sufficiently vigorous to break loose from the nest in sufficient quantities that the male can no longer keep them together, he does not attempt it, but concerns himself solely with endeavors to keep the youngsters in something resembling a school, only retrieving and returning those that venture too far away from the main group. The babies may be under their father's care for three weeks, but are usually ignored or eaten when they are about twelve days old. It is by no means unusual, however, to find a male fish which will eat the babies as soon as they are hatched, or one which will even eat the eggs; so, as usual, we cannot say that any one fish will nurse its babies for any definite length of time. The only way to make sure that a few of the fry escape the fate of being suddenly turned into a large fish through the intermediary of their father's jaws is to watch carefully and to remove the large fish as soon as he shows any signs of infanticide.

These fish are technically called *Betta splendens,* and there are almost as many varieties as there are of Goldfish, for they are given to a certain amount of freakishness in the babies, which fact has been seized upon by aquarists who select the most extraordinary of the babies for intensive breeding. Any wild fish which is not of a sufficiently great beauty, either of color or form, to warrant its inclusion in an aquarium of lovely fishes, may be the parent of fishes which develop long fins, or excessive amounts of one or another color. If these fishes are taken out and bred together, the young resulting will, in obedience to Mendel's Law, tend toward the color or shape of their parents. After several generations of such selective breeding, the strain may be fairly fixed, but as the wild unlovely fish may be the parent of beautifully colored and finned specimens, so does the selected stock produce babies which revert to the shape and color of the original great-grandparents. These are known as "culls" and have little or no market value.

The female of this species is slightly smaller than the male, but well-grown specimens of both sexes approach two and a half inches in length. The colors of both are ordinarily similar, and are not prepossessing. Over a dull grayish-brown body there are a few dark stripes—sometimes two and sometimes three. These are crossed not infrequently, with bars of the same general color. There is, however, a suggestion of brick-red, blue or green, or a combination of these, all over the body, which is particularly evident when the fish are breeding. There are also a number of green spots scattered over the body, although these are not always visible. The fins are small, and there are vague hints that under the dark color there may be other, brighter hues. These colors, at the mating time, are more than hints, but are always obscured somewhat by the general brownness of the body. However, a metallic green shade is observable in the dorsal fin, and the anal fin is tinted with blue or red. The tail fin is similar, usually, to the anal in color, but even at the best of times, the fish is dark, and has the appearance of being best suited to murky water where it would not be easily picked out of its surroundings. I have mentioned this coloration in some detail for a definite reason, for it is on these colors that those of the gorgeous Fighting Fish of the pet stores, with their flowing fins of red, scarlet, green, blue, maroon, are based. Whatever the color of the fancy specimen, there is a root color in the wild type, undeveloped and dormant, but nevertheless ready to burst forth in all its glory when the fish wearing such a livery has a remote chance of escaping the eyes of fish-eaters, all too soon attracted by such a color. Where the large fins come from, I have no idea. The fins of the wild type are small—entirely suitable to the size of the body—while the most desired of aquarium-bred stock have fins each of which is as large or larger than the body which bears them. It is worthy of note that the colors of the wild specimens deepen and intensify considerably during the breeding time, although the colors of the aquarium stock are fixed at all times. Two or three years ago, really good specimens of aquarium-raised *Betta splendens* were quite expensive, as much as thirty dollars being paid for one pair. Now they are much more reasonable in price.

It is curious, but entirely to be expected, that fishes which are so heavily finned will seldom fight, although they will nip each other and spoil the fins by tearing bits off them. However, the weight of such trailing drapery must be considerable, and quite sufficient to hinder any great ambition for suitably maintaining the fighting tradition of his ancestry.

Torn and mutilated fins usually will regenerate, but there is almost always a slight wave or ripple across the rays of the fin caused by the scar tissue. This spoils the appearance of the fish; for this reason promising youngsters should be kept in isolation as they grow if clean clear sweeps of fins are desired. It hardly ever happens that a single fish of a family of young ones is not bitten at one time or another by his brothers, and the fins will never be really attractive. This isolation is not very difficult, for the fish is so constituted that it can live and grow to a good size in a small aquarium. Many splendid males have been reared in fish bowls scarcely larger than an ordinary tumbler.

There is a cream-colored strain, in which the fins may be any of the basic colors to the *n*th degree, which is called *Betta cambodia*. The fish is a true *Betta splendens*, but the name "Cambodia" serves to identify the specific color, and is quite useful in that respect, although it is scientifically incorrect. The other types have been variously referred to as the "Loie

Fuller Fish," the "Corn-flower Blue," "Smaragdgreen," "Veil-tail," and other more or less descriptive names. However, the tendency today is to refer to the fish as plain "Betta," or "Fighting Fish," preceded by the name of the color.

## II. Nests and Courting

The nests these fish build are curious structures whose composition is not well understood. Almost all the members of the family build the typical nest or a variation of it, either in location or in the materials used.

All but one of the Bettas (*Betta pugnax*)—there are several species in the genus, although almost none but *splendens* has ever been recorded as arriving here—the Paradise Fishes and some of the Gouramies build the same kind of nest in approximately the same location. The methods of fertilizing the eggs as they are liberated are substantially the same, too.

All of these fishes are able to breathe atmospheric air, mouthfuls of which are taken periodically and stored in a cavity above the gills. They can absorb the oxygen from water, too, a useful trick for some of our more amphibiously minded athletes to learn.

Whether these fishes are only able to use air directly in extreme youth, and have no workable gills with which to take the necessary oxygen from the water, or whether it is, or was at one time, necessary for the eggs to develop at the surface, we do not know. We do know that the eggs are carefully placed among the bubbles of air made by the male parent, and that they are hatched there.

These bubbles are small quantities of air taken in the mouth of the fish and liberated at the surface of the water. They are coated with a mucous secretion which makes them slightly adhesive, and they are made and released in such numbers as to make a fairly large "raft" several inches across. The raft is usually attached to the side of the aquarium or to a leaf of plant, or, if there are any floating leaves of a large enough size, under the leaf. At the center there may be a small mound caused by the male concentrating his bubbles in one place. Masses of bubbles have been lifted from the aquarium in which they were made and placed elsewhere, without any apparent damage to the contents, but unless we know exactly how many eggs were fertilized, and how many hatch, an almost impossible requirement, we will never know just what the exact methods of incubation are, for in spite of popular opinion, eggs are usually pretty viable things which require considerable abuse to destroy. They get this quite frequently, more through ignorance than anything else, but since no one knows just what are correct conditions and what not, I do not think anything can be done about it.

After the nest is formed, the male attracts the eye of a female by spreading his fins to their utmost and vibrating them slightly. He also bows and gestures continually until the female is enticed below the nest. Then there is an embrace, in which the male bends himself about the female, the vents of both fishes almost touching. During this embrace, a few eggs are liberated, perhaps a dozen, but as few as four or five sometimes. Then the fishes part; the female to right herself—she has been thrown off an even keel by the activity—and the male to pick up the eggs in his mouth. He carries them up to the nest and shoots them in with some little force. Then the fish embrace again, with a fine quivering of bodies and fins. After each embrace the eggs which are released and which sink slowly toward the bottom of the water are retrieved by the male and installed in the nest. This procedure may go on for hours, until perhaps five hundred eggs are in place, and then the male, surfeited, drives off the female and assumes the duty of watching that the eggs do not break their moorings and fall from the nest. If the female stays within range of the male, she may be killed; certainly she will be badly beaten. If she can secure any eggs, she will, in a weak and inefficient manner, thereafter attend to them herself in a small nest of her own building. If there is a bit of stone that makes a sort of cave, and the male is sufficiently vicious, the female will retire into the shadow of the stone, venturing forth only to take an occasional mouthful of air and to snap up an egg which may fall within reach.

Curiously, the eggs which the female will protect at the bottom of a tank seem to develop into just as strong and healthy little fishes as the ones which had a more normal rearing. It has also been observed that the fishes, if given any preference about the depth of water over which they may build the nest, frequently pick the shallowest part as the site, but fishes confined in large deep tanks have quite successfully raised families too; so it is doubtful if the depth of water has any definite bearing on the growth or well being of the young fish. It may be a matter of protection, for a fish in water just deep enough to float him will have fewer fronts on which he may be attacked, always assuming that there is some sort of cover overhead, which, according to numberless observations, seems to be the case, for the fishes will invariably build their nests under large floating leaves, if any are available. However, our aquarium-bred Bettas may be developing aquarium preferences by now—there have been raised many generations under innumerable changes of conditions in aquaria, and wild specimens are decidedly rare—so changes in the site chosen may be in the making at this time.

The embrace mentioned a little while ago has been the subject of considerable discussion. The theory that force is actually used by the male during the liberation of the eggs by the female has been advanced and has some superficial foundation. However, such an idea is hardly sound if general biological knowledge is considered, nor is it sound mechanically, for the strength necessary to get any force at all between two primary levers such as the fish turns himself into during the embrace is beyond all reasonableness.

There is a theory that the young of these fishes will drown if the parent does not replace them in the nest every time they fall out, but while this may be so in many cases, several filled nests have been robbed of their guardians without complete disaster descending on the youngsters who grew up to be perfectly normal fishes.

If a number of fish are kept together in a large aquarium, males may be observed building nests for the accommodation of the eggs of more than one female, making one at a time, looking after it for a few days, and then abandoning it to build another one for another female. As many as four nests with eggs in each have been observed at the same time—all the product of a single male, which seems to have an unlimited capacity to spawn. The females are not quite so prolific, usually not spawning more frequently than once every two or three weeks for a period of a month or two. The "season" during which these fish breed is not constant at all. Any time in the year is just as good as any other, as far as aquarium observations show, for there are baby fish and half-grown ones and full-grown ones available at all times.

As with the Fighting Fish, so with the Paradise Fishes.

## III. Paradise Fishes

There are at least three different species of these: the Fork-tailed Paradise Fish, *Macropodus opercularis* from Indo-China; the Round-tailed Paradise Fish, *Macropodus chinensis* from China and Korea; and the Sharp-tailed Paradise Fish, *Macropodus cupanus,* from pretty near all of Southern and Eastern Asia. The latter is represented in two different strains, only one of which is popular in aquaria. This is given the variety name of *Macropodus cupanus dayi,* and averages about two and three-quarter inches long—half an inch longer than the type species. However, since the ranges of the two types are about the same, it is now supposed that they are only genetical strains and not different species, as at one time listed.

The breeding and attendance of the young of all the Paradise Fishes is similar to that of the Fighting Fish, but occasionally a specimen of the Sharp-tailed species may be found which will build the bubble nest under the overhanging ledge of a bit of stone or shell. If, in the case of the latter, the amount of air carried down is large and the imprisoned bubbles overturn the shell and spill out the nest, it immediately floats to the surface.

As the names indicate, there is considerable difference in the shapes of the tails of the different species; otherwise they are similar in color and appearance. They are all lovely fish of a brownish body, over which are striped dark bars and bands. These may be of blue or red or the colors may alternate. There is considerable spotting of small dots of black or light shining colors, or very dark blue, and considerable variation in the colors of different specimens. The behavior in general is the same—willingness to fight with all comers. This should be always borne in mind when dealing with these fishes, although an occasional specimen is found which will not bother anything.

This is more pronounced in the Sharp-tailed Paradise, but they are never to be trusted, for they may develop atavistic streaks at any moment.

The Fork-tailed Paradise has long fins, much as the aquarium-bred Fighting Fish, and has the honor of being the first tropical fish ever shipped into colder countries as a domestic pet. This occurred in 1869, when a French military attaché discovered the charming colors and interesting behavior of the fish, and sent a few pair home to France. Since then they have traveled to all countries where pets are maintained, and have achieved an amazing popularity. This, however, is somewhat dimmed at present because of the availability of so many other species of fishes of equal beauty but more peaceful manners.

However, no aquarist should fail to keep a pair of one or another kind of these fishes at some time, for the habits are really so interesting and unexpected that much is lost if one only has second-hand knowledge of them.

These fishes are very hardy, and are really semi-tropical in the temperature of the water they tolerate, for they may all be kept in good health even when the water temperature falls as low as sixty degrees. They will also tolerate quite high temperatures, in addition to their ability to withstand the rigors and disasters consequent upon the water becoming foul. This latter is because they are independent of the water for breathing purposes. When it becomes too thick and polluted for the exercise of ordinary gills and when ordinary fishes would suffocate, these fishes are quite at home.

## IV. The Gouramies

There are other fish in this family which build bubble nests. All the Gouramies are in this category, but they do not all use exactly the same methods. Some species of this genus are very popular, being among the most beautiful of all fishes, and some of them very peaceful, in contradistinction to many of their cousins.

The best known of the Gouramies is the Three-spot. This is a little differently colored from most of its relatives, being predominantly a silvery brown. There are only two spots, one on the side, about the center, and one at the base of the tail. These are large, dark and distinct. The third spot is probably the very obvious eye. All over the body are fine wavy lines, sloping from the back downward and slightly forward, making for a very attractive appearance. *Trichogaster trichopterus,* the scientific name of the Three-spot, builds a nest in manner almost identical with those of the Paradise and Fighting Fishes, although the eggs are supposed to be lighter than water, consequently rising after they are liberated instead of sinking as with all the others. The male pays both the eggs and the young fish the same kind and amount of attention as the other two nest-building genera. The eggs take about the same time to hatch and the young leave the nest at about the same age, from one to three days and about four days, respectively. However, there is a marked difference in body structure between this fish and others of the same habits. The ventral fins of the Bettas are small affairs, not particularly noticeable. Those of the Paradise are small too, but there is a short wisp, a pale yellow in color, growing from the end of the ventrals of the Fork-tailed Paradise. The same fins in the Gouramies, however, are prolonged until they reach the tail almost,—slender, pale yellow, feeler-like structures apparent at a glance, and thickening at the base where they join the body. These are in constant motion, moving about in all directions, and the fish uses them extensively, investigating with them almost every object with which he comes into contact. Both sexes possess them, and they are characteristic of the Gouramies generally.

The Three-spot is a peaceful fish, fairly large for an aquarium. However, his ability to breathe atmospheric air makes him suitable for a small aquarium, much too small for other fishes of the same length. Good specimens reach five inches long, both sexes being of about the same size and general appearance. Apart from a border of red spots on the anal and dorsal fins of the male, there is no external difference visible.

This fish has also been called the Hair-fin Gourami, an appropriate name. It is found in the waters of the Malay Peninsula as far north as Southern China, and is very readily bred in domestic aquaria.

A fish somewhat smaller than the Three-spot, but with similar markings, is the Banded Gourami. This fellow is about four inches long when full grown, and has about the same general body color as the larger one. The stripes, however, are much more distinct, and are sloped the other way. They are also much more highly colored, and may be either red or blue. This, the *Colisa fasciata,* decided that Northern India and the countries immediately adjacent to the eastward would be a good place to live; so all our specimens originated there. Their breeding, about the same as the others, is not the least inhibited by life in the aquarium. There is a marked difference between the sexes. The male is much more highly colored than the female, and the dorsal fin is pointed. Hers is round at the end. The ventral fins of this species are developed much as those of the Three-spot, and are used in a similar manner. There is a difference in the color of these fins. The male ventrals are yellowish, and the female white, but such a difference is not at once apparent, and is more comparative than the other distinctions.

A smaller fish with much more color than either of its immediate relatives is the Dwarf Gourami, *Colisa lalia.* This species has a much deeper body than is usual in the group, and is exceptionally highly colored in alternate stripes of blue and red. These stripes slope backward from the back of the fish, and are slender and clear-cut. Individuals of this species are small, about two inches long, and very retiring, preferring the shelter of aquatic plants to open water. They make a bubble nest too, which floats at the surface of the water, but these, instead of trusting to the stickiness of the bubbles to hold together the raft, interlace bits of plant leaves among the bubbles. Whether this has anything to do with the fact that the fish eat a good deal of vegetation is problematic, but we do not know of any other fish which does such a thing and is not also a vegetarian to a certain extent.

The range of this species is identical with that of the last, Assam, Borneo, Upper Burma, and Northern India, all being countries of origin, as the Customs Service likes to know.

There are no definite secondary sex characters. Except that the male is brighter in color, it is almost impossible to distinguish male from female. These fishes are very peaceful, and add color and variety to an aquarium.

There is a Gourami whose claim to fame is not in its beauty nor habits, which are almost identical with those of the last-named species. It is about the same size or a little larger—perhaps two and a half inches long—but not nearly so lovely to look at. It has a certain popularity in its own right, however, based on its voice! Some fishes have voices of one sort or other, but this one, the Croaking Gourami of the Malayan Peninsula, is the only one of this kind kept in aquaria. It is, however, very rare, and is only encountered in the tanks of the most assiduous collectors of fishes. During the breeding period, when the male is courting, and when he is looking after the eggs, he makes a small noise remotely resembling the purring of a happy cat. The noise is not very loud and could easily be missed by anyone not familiar with the habits of the fish. The female has not been reported as having any voice at all, and it is not very well understood how the male fish makes the noise, or why, but it is sufficiently interesting to make the fish well worth acquiring, should the opportunity arise. The fish is not a true Gourami, belonging to a different genus, but he builds a nest similar to that of the Dwarf Gourami, even using the bits of plants in its construction. The eggs hatch about four days after they are thrust into the nest, and the care of the young by the male is similar to most of the others of the group. The males, besides the peculiar noise they make, are quite easily distinguished from the females. The colors of both are more or less alike, with the usual difference that the brightest are carried by the male. The fins are noticeably different, those of the male being quite long against the short ones of the female. This fish, *Ctenops vittatus,* is of the same general body color as most of the Gouramies, a reddish brown, although he may look as if he were blue in certain lights. He differs in that the light lines over the bodies of the Gouramies are concentrated, in this species, into several fairly heavy lines which run from the head to the tail. Sometimes three of these lines are visible, and sometimes four, and sometimes the lines do not run right through to the tail, but end half way down the body. They are all there, probably, but are visible or not according to the condition of the fish.

The Croaking Gourami is very peaceful and is quite suitable for inclusion in a tank of other fishes.

Another peaceful fish of the same general group is the Thick-lipped Gourami, *Colisa labiosa*. This one gets his odd name from the noticeably swollen lips of the male, which are very obvious. The female does not exhibit any peculiarity of the lips, but instead has a more conspicuous line running from her nose to the beginning of the tail. This is also visible, but to a much lesser degree, on the sides of the male. About three, or three and a half inches long, the Thick-lipped Gourami is very attractive, marked as he is with about ten or twelve bright red lines across the greenish sides. (It is difficult to describe the colors of fishes, for they are usually a complicated mixture of shades, one of which is more pronounced that the others, according to the light in which they are viewed. In a different light, another color may be more noticeable. In this case, the same specimen may look reddish brown at one minute, and a pale yellowish green at another, in exactly the same light, the difference being due to the ever-changing angles from the light source at which the fish places himself as he swims about the tank.) The dark spot at the base of the tail is very conspicuous and appears to be dark blue or black. The fins, which may show a red line at the edge, are one of the shades of green. Altogether, a charming color scheme.

The building of the nest and the care of the young are almost identical with those of most of the other Gouramies. This fish does not use bits of leaves, as far as we know. Its habitat is Burma and the states to the eastward—a true Asiatic.

There are two fishes of this family which are not aquarium fishes, but their habits differ so from those of most of the family that they may well be mentioned. The first, a Gourami, is too large for ordinary aquarium culture, being about two feet long. He, too, builds a nest of air bubbles, but this is built at the bottom of the water, among the stalks of reeds, to which the nest is anchored. The nest is globular in shape, and is built in proportion to his size. Our reasoning tells us that this nest would be much too obvious for the rearing of young fishes inside, for while most of these fishes are less than six inches, they build rafts of bubbles which may be six inches across. A small nest like this is noticeable, but if the two-foot-long Gourami built his at the surface, it would be a fine advertisement of the eggs beneath to the numberless wild things that would enjoy them. However, we do not know that the Gourami reasons as we do, or even at all; so just why the large nest is built away out of sight is something that is yet to be discovered.

We do not know why any of the nests are built yet. Whether it is because the young must have air, or whether it is because they are readily attacked by the fungi and molds which may be unable to penetrate through the mass of bubbles, or whether there are yet other reasons, we have not the slightest inkling.

The other fish of the family is a Betta, *Betta pugnax*—another fighting name. This fish comes from Singapore and Malacca, and, as far as size goes, he is quite suitable for aquarium life, for he is not above three inches long. There are other difficulties about which we know nothing. He lives in swiftly running water and may be suitable for a flowing water aquarium such as many Goldfish are kept in. Since he lives in running water, a nest of bubbles would be most unsuitable, for such fragile affairs are easily carried away, or broken up at least, for the only thing that holds them together is the slight stickiness of the bubbles themselves, except where the fish uses bits of leaves when the bubbles stick to the vegetation as well. The fish overcomes this difficulty by adopting the methods of some of the African Cichlids, which use their mouths as incubation chambers. After the eggs are spawned and fertilized, the female is reputed to pick them up in her mouth and carry them about until they are hatched. Some authorities claim that it is the male who carries the eggs, a fact which may be borne out by the actions of the males of the other species which are so solicitous of their young. However, we know that the females of even these species will attend to the eggs if they can get them. It may therefore well be that both sexes of the Singapore Fighting Fish carry the eggs in their mouths, sharing the responsibility as do many of the Cichlids. The most recent observations indicate that both sexes carry the eggs, but the male takes the majority of them.

There is a frog which lives in Central America. This frog makes nests which are very similar in appearance to those of the Labyrinth Fish and are probably of similar materials. Sometimes the pools in which the frog lives are dried up, and then the nest with its complement of eggs is left high and dry. They have been encountered many yards from the nearest water, sometimes a mile away, but when they are opened, the tiny tadpoles, which have hatched from the eggs, are swimming vigorously, and apparently healthily, in the liquid enclosed in the mass. When the rains come again and fill up all the little pools, the nest is probably broken up and the young tadpoles released. There may be some such idea back of the building of the nests of these fishes.

## V. The Climbing Perch

There are a few more fishes related to these Bettas and Gouramis and Paradise Fish which share with them the ability to breathe air. One, at least, is frequently encountered in aquaria and is quite a famous fish, having been talked of and written about for the past hundred years or more. This is the famous Climbing Perch of China. He comes from India, too, but is more popularly known as a Chinese. His fame lies in the fact that he can live long periods without water and can and does wriggle about overland quite effectively, but his reputation was established on a much more astounding basis. The fish is reputed to climb trees. Just why he should, no one seems to know. Nor has anyone ever seen him climbing a tree, but he has been found up trees occasionally, probably having been carried there by a bird and wriggling loose before he was eaten. However he got there, no one knows, for the fish has no legs or anything remotely approaching legs which would enable him to climb or even walk. What he has, and what he uses in his meanderings about the land, are some spines which grow on the edge of the opercle—the bony covering of the gills. These lie flat along the side of the fish when he is in the water, but when he wants to move from one place to another between which there is no water, he extends these gill-covers until they are sticking out at about right angles to his body. Using these as levers, he moves the pectoral fins and tail vigorously, and is so able to progress across fairly uneven ground. By no stretch of the imagination could he use these for climbing very steep or smooth surfaces, for the spines are in a plane across the body, and are not very flexible, if at all. However, the Climbing Perch seems to be firmly established in history, and he certainly may be established in aquaria just as firmly, if anyone is interested, for he is hardy and requires little care or space. His air-breathing apparatus enables him to live where other fishes, except his near relatives, would suffocate, and as long as he has little more water than will keep him wet, he seems happy. His name is *Anabas testudineus,* and his range extends from Southern China on the north to the islands off the north coast of Australia on the south. The eastward boundary is about the Philippines, and the westward, India.

This fish, although he belongs to the air-breathing and nest-building family, does not make a nest but deposits eggs near the surface of the water on which they float in a more or less compact mass. Whether or not he pays them any attention afterward is doubtful, but it is quite possible in the wild state. Aquarium fish are not longer than about five inches, but full-grown wild ones are at least twice that. They are not brightly colored, being of a more or less light-brown monotone, but the fins are darker. The sexual characteristics are not very evident, to us at least, but they must be fully recognizable by the fishes themselves, for if more than one of each sex are kept together, the largest of the one sex will kill or drive off the smaller, no matter what sex it is. A pair of fish seem to live in perfect amity, even through they never spawn.

There are two other Climbing Perches, both from Africa. Neither of these arrives in our aquaria, although on a comparison of size, they are more suitable than the one from India. The largest of these is the one from the waters of the Niger, *Ctenopoma argentoventer.* This, about six inches long, is similar in habits and appearance to the Indian Perch. The smaller African species is much better-looking. It only reaches a length of about three inches, and is similar to the Paradise Fish in appearance. This one is called *Ctenopoma fasciolatus,* and inhabits the Congo River and its tributaries. Just why this fish has never become popular is one of the minor mysteries of tropical fish culture. The fish is colorful, easily kept and not over large, but is hardly ever brought in. His rarity might be taken into account, if it were not for the fact that many other fishes, equally rare, have now been successfully established. Perhaps the natives of his homeland are so busy maintaining themselves that they have neither the time nor the urge to bother about the cultural possibilities of a fish too small to be eaten with any satisfaction.

# Chapter 10

## The Killies

THIS FAMILY of fishes is the most widespread of any treated here. There are many members, coming from practically all of the known world, with the possible exception of Australasia and the Arctic and Antarctic regions. Most of the representatives of the family that are kept as domestic pets are freshwater species, but there are a few brackish-water fishes, and even a few from ocean water, although these latter are in a very definite minority. The brackish-water fishes have to go through a longer or shorter period of adjustment before they can be truly called aquarium fishes.

Most of the family are very lovely little fishes, and as they are all fairly hardy and peacefully disposed, and not impossible to breed in the aquarium, they are all more or less popular. They are not all tropical fishes, of course, but their adaptability is such that even fishes from the coastal waters of North America may adjust themselves sufficiently to live in the cramped quarters and fresh water of the domestic aquarium. One unscrupulous dealer in aquarium fishes discovered this years ago and built up a fine business selling as tropical fish from Africa the common Killie from the coast of Long Island. The record is not quite clear about the species, but it was either *Fundulus heteroclitus* or *Cyprinodon variegatus*, both beautiful little fishes entitled to a place in the aquarium in their own right, but now banished since the deception was discovered.

All of these fishes spawn freely—at least all of the aquarium species do, if they are given anything remotely resembling decent conditions, but the eggs take some time to hatch, and many are undoubtedly lost to the aquarist through impatience. This is hardly to be wondered at, for the eggs of the vast majority of aquarium fishes hatch in two or three days—less than a week, anyway—while the eggs of the Killie Fishes may take as long as three weeks. The unwary aquarist, expecting to see young from a pair of fishes he has placed together in the aquarium a week or so later, becomes discouraged when none is visible, and turns the tank over to other uses, thus losing any eggs there may be.

At least one of the species is remarkable in the viability of its eggs. If a pair of *Panchax chaperi* are kept in an aquarium into which the net goes occasionally, or from which plants are taken to stock another tank, baby Chaperis will begin to show up in the most unexpected places. The eggs are slightly adhesive and, sticking to the net, are transferred to other tanks, where they seem to develop without exception, although the conditions of the water may be as different as it is possible for them to be and still have fishes live in it.

## I. Aphyosemion

The most colorful of these fishes are those from West Africa, although they are not necessarily the most beautiful. These are the species of the genus *Aphyosemion*, to which the lovely Lyretail belongs. This fish, probably the most expensive of ordinary, available fishes, originated in Liberia, but almost all of the specimens now offered in the dealers' stores are of American birth. It is not quite as hardy under adverse conditions as most of its cousins, but if given an aquarium in which there is not too great a variation in temperature, and a supply of such floating plants as the Lesser Bladderwort, Crystalwort or Myriophyllum, it will be quite happy, and will shed eggs in a fairly steady stream. These are attached to the floating plants, and are fairly large and clear. They hatch in two weeks, or perhaps a few days less, but they do not always achieve maturity, for the young fish are not as hardy as their parents, and cannot tolerate any changes of conditions, seemingly—a fact which is regrettable but beyond the control of most aquarists.

The colors of the fish are vivid and attractive, the male as usual being the most highly decorated.

Like the rest of his genus, this fish is of a peculiarly retiring disposition, he much prefers lying quietly among a thicket of floating plants with the head only showing than to just plain swimming. He reminds one of a rather shy mouse who knows that there is a piece of cheese near by, and no cats about, but who sits inside his hole looking out for a long time before he ventures out to get the cheese. If he thinks he is observed, he vanishes in a flash. The Lyretail seems to do just that. His head, if one looks closely about the tank, may be seen poking out of the leaves or from behind a clump of stalks, although the other fishes in the tank are disporting themselves in perfect faith in the perpetual peace of the aquarium. When the fish does show himself, one wonders why such a beauty should be so bashful, for he is at least the equal, and usually the best-looking, of any of our aquarium fishes.

The colors of the body are a light brown, blending into a bluish green behind the gills. Several series of red dots run down the length of the body, those nearer the head being so close together that they give the impression of solid lines. The red-spotted dorsal fin of the male is fringed with white, next to which is a dark line. The anal fin, light blue in color, is edged with yellow outside a dark red line. Both of these fins are pointed at the end and may have streamers from the extremity. The ventrals are similar to the anal, and the pectoral fins are light blue. The tail fin has the most fancy markings, however. The base color is a bluish green, with a slightly curved dark-red line on each lobe. Above the upper line is another line of white or yellow, and below the lower line is an edging of bright orange red. The greenish part of the tail is marked with dark-red dots and lines, and the whole effect is that of an ancient lyre, the dark lines making the sides, and the dots and inner lines making the strings. This gay appearance is further heightened by the shape of the tail, in which the outside rays are prolonged into streamers, and the center ones are also lengthened, but not to the same extent as the outer ones. The female is not nearly so bright. She is of the same general body color, but the lines and spots are not as clearly marked as those of her mate. The fins too are of a different shape, being more or less round at the ends, and of a pale-green color. There are a few red spots on the dorsal and tail fins, but these are barely noticeable.

It is not essential that the eggs of this species be removed from the tank in which they are deposited, for mature fish are very mild and peaceful and do not eat them. However, the temptation to try one or two of the wriggling larvæ, when the eggs hatch, usually proves too much for any fish. If babies are wanted, it is safer to remove the plants to which the eggs adhere to another tank, where they may be left undisturbed for several weeks after they have hatched.

The popular name, which seems to die hard, is Cameronensis, and although scientifically it is wrong, the fish will be readily identified by anyone with the slightest knowledge of fishes by that name.

There is a fish which carries that name by right, but it is almost unknown outside the pickled collections of museums and places of that nature. This one, *Aphyosemion cameronensis,* is slightly greener than the Lyretail, but is otherwise of a generally similar color. However, these differ considerably in different specimens. The tails of both sexes are round, too, instead of the three lobes of the pretender to the title *Cameronensis*.

There is one fish, a near relative, from the regions of Africa to the south and east of the habitat of the Lyretail. This is *Aphyosemion australe,* popularly called Cape Lopez, and from that so-named cape in the Gabun. In appearance, this fish is very similar to the Lyretail, having substantially the same colors, although the brown of the body is more chocolaty than the brown of the Lyretail. The same shape of tail and style of fins complete the likeness, but the fish is of a somewhat slighter build. The size is about the same in both species—two inches or so—as are the habits. This fish is the one most available, and is sometimes called Cameronensis too. It is not entirely clear how the amateur is to distinguish among the species, but since they are of a comparable loveliness, I suppose it does not really matter.

There are other fishes from the same general locality of a similar shape; that is, the males have points to their tails and dorsal and anal fins while the female has plain round ends, but their colors are not to be compared with those of the various fishes called Cameronensis. Some of these, such as *Aphyosemion bitæniatus,* a yellowish fish from the Niger region, and *Aphyosemion gardneri,* a blue fish from the same place or a little further east, almost to the Cameroon, and *Aphyosemion arnoldi,* a fish the upper part of which is brownish yellow and the lower a dark blue, from the delta of the Niger, occasionally find their way into the stores of the dealers, but there are never many, and those that do arrive, unfortunately, do not seem to thrive in the water of the New World. They are all attractive fishes, of approximately the same breeding habits, and if an aquarist should succeed in rearing a few, he would be well repaid by the splendid show they would make.

One red relative of these fishes is *Aphyosemion sjæstedti.* The head of this fish presents a wonderful array of color. The top is green, the lip bright red, the gill-covers and throat dark blue, the space between the eye and the gill-covers spotted and lined with red, which continues over the blue of the latter. A bright golden line runs from the gills to just below the dorsal fin.

The fins are all different too. The dorsal is blue at the top, red at the base and is covered with red dots. The pectoral fins are green, with red edges. The ventrals yellowish green. The anal fin deep blue with red spots along the base. The upper part of the tail is blue, the lower yellow or white, with a line or two of deep blue. In spite of this bewildering array of color, the general appearance of the fish is that it is red, so intense are the red lines and dots along the sides.

Specimens of this species are frequently available in the fish stores, although they are not common fishes by any means.

The fish hails from the coasts of the Gulf of Guinea, and is a really beautiful creature.

The breeding is about the same as that of the other species of the same genus, but it is never safe to say that any fish always breeds in such and such a manner, for the specific differences are always great, and sometimes, for no apparent reason at all, one specimen of a species will vary his habits considerably. For instance, many fishes which habitually deposit their eggs among floating plants, as does *Aphyosemion sjæstedti,* will suddenly spawn at the bottom of the water among the débris or even on clear sand, after sweeping the sediment away with its fins. The young hatch in approximately the same numbers in either place. When a fish is supposed to deposit eggs in leaves at the top of the water, do not be angry and call down the wrath of high heaven upon the fellow who told you it would, if you find your specimen placing its eggs at the bottom. Both places may be perfectly normal for the conditions obtaining in your respective aquaria.

A few more of this genus of fishes are available. Among them are *Aphyosemion gularis,* known as the Yellow Gularis, because of the predominant color. This fish, like its relatives, has a complicated pattern of lines and dots, most of which are of one or other shade of brown or yellow. This is from the northeastern corner of the Gulf of Guinea, particularly about the Niger Delta, and is one of the fishes which is reported as habitually depositing its eggs in the débris at the bottom of the tank. These eggs are, however, large and adhesive, so if you should find any stuck to leaves in your aquarium, do not be surprised.

Another Gularis, blue this time, is called *Aphyosemion cœruleus* and comes from the same regions as the yellow one. This has pretty much the same pattern—done in blue, as the name suggests—and habits as its yellow relative. This fish reaches a length of about five inches, twice as long as the last, and is somewhat more frequently encountered.

Many of these fishes have been listed under the generic name *Fundulopanchax,* but have recently been straightened out in nomenclature and placed in the genus *Aphyosemion.* Their specific names, according to the best authorities, are still in a state of flux and are much too indefinite to be argued about. It is possible that the species were quite clear and distinct at one time but have bred together and resulted in our fishes. No crossings between the species are reported in aquaria, however.

In general, the Fundulopanchax were always supposed by aquarists to spawn at the bottom of the water, while the Aphyosemion were limited to the top, but no such artificial differentiation can safely be made, as we said before, for fishes change their habits frequently. However, they all deposit eggs over a fairly long period, several hundred, perhaps being spawned at the rate of a few a day for two or three weeks, and the eggs all take from ten to twenty days to hatch. None of these fishes is pugnacious, being apparently quite happy with any number of other kinds, as long as the others do not molest them. If they do, these will not fight back, but will probably be killed. If you have any of them and value them, do not tempt Providence by leaving a bully in the aquarium.

## II. Panchaxes

Related to this group of fishes is another which is not only of African, but also of Asiatic, origin. This is the *Panchax* group. Many of them are quite lovely, and are more commonly kept in aquaria than the last group. A few come from West Africa, but all but one of them are comparatively unknown in North America. The exception is probably the best known of the whole group. This is *Panchax chaperi,* from Sierra Leone, Liberia, the Ivory Coast and the Gold Coast. This fish is about two and a half inches long when fully grown, and is an amazingly prolific breeder. The males are the brightest in color, and have more decorations, for the ends of the anal, dorsal and caudal fins are extended into streamers. The ventral fins are also somewhat longer than those of the female. In addition, the fins especially the anal and tail, are marked with dark bars. The chin of the male is a bright scarlet. Both sexes carry about six distinctly marked black bars on their sides. However, the general impression is not one of color, but of a black and white fish. This is a peaceful species, content to take up a position beneath a few leaves and to stay there all day and all night, unless there is something in the way of food to induce a little action. It does swim about occasionally, however, and presents a rather quiet attractiveness.

The eggs are liberated in much the same manner as in many of the Aphyosemion; that is, they are deposited in small numbers in the close leaves of floating plants. A number are liberated every day for quite a long period, and the breeders of such fishes usually use one of two methods of preserving the eggs. They either set up a battery of small jars or tanks, each with a bunch of Myriophyllum or Nitella or some such plant, and place one pair of the fishes in the first jar for a few days, and then move them to the next. In this way, all of the jars will possibly contain a few eggs which are not touched then for several weeks. The young fish, if any materialize, are fed on very finely ground fish foods, or on a few teaspoonfuls of an infusoria culture. The other method in common use is to place a pair of the fish in a fairly large tank with a quantity of the same kind of plant, and change the plant every few days, placing it in a clean jar, and putting fresh plants in with the fish. The results are the same. There are a few eggs in each small jar. Of course, the plant does not have to be moved. If the fish are healthy and well fed, the plant need never be moved, for the eggs will hatch right in the aquarium with the parents. These eggs take about two weeks to hatch.

It is a curious fact that in aquaria proportionately very few males develop from the eggs. In some instances as few as three males to almost a thousand females have resulted from several spawnings. Whether this is due to purely aquarium conditions, in which a differential viability in favor of the females is sometimes evident, or is about the same ratio as occurs in nature, no one seems to know. Such a small ratio of males is not always the case, of course, but all breeders report the same large majority of females, although the actual numbers vary considerably.

Neighbors of the Chaperi in its habitat—almost all the Panchaxes reported from Africa as suitable aquarium fishes come from the same general locality, the countries bordering the Gulf of Guinea, which is quite a large stretch of country, but small compared to the rest of Africa—are not very well known.

There is *Panchax grahami* from Southern Nigeria. About two inches long, it does not seem to have any definite color scheme. Some specimens have a few—about six—dark bars across the body. Others have red spots in lines running down the body. Still others have both series of lines, while some may have any one or both of these color patterns with red dots on their fins. In general, however, it is usually the male which carries the spotted tail. The body color is a yellowish brown; the lips are red and there is a bluish spot on the side of the head. The female has the same variable pattern, but is not nearly as brilliantly marked as the male, which is not especially noteworthy for its markings itself.

Another two-inch Panchax from the same place is *Panchax longiventralis*. This too does not seem to be quite decided about its colors, for some specimens are spotted with red and others are not. The tendency to spots is much more marked in the male than in the female, as is the tendency to be barred with long narrow dots of brown or red along the lower part of the sides. The sexes may be more distinctly distinguished by the clear fins of the female; those of the male are inclined to green, with a few spots of red scattered about them.

From Liberia down to the Congo comes another Panchax which is really very good-looking. This is *Panchax sexfasciatus*. It is about four inches long and is banded with half a dozen black lines, some of which do not quite reach around the body. Between the lines there are other blotches and spots of black. These stand out well against the yellowish body, although the yellow runs the gamut of possible shades of that color. (All the Panchaxes seem to be hesitant about the color they will present to the world. Perhaps they have the power to change their colors at will, but lose it when they are captured and have to stay the color they were when they were caught!) However, most of the Banded Panchaxes have a profusion of red dots scattered about the body, and the males are further decorated by the delicate lemon-colored fins. These are edged with black. The female has no color in her fins.

The eggs of these fishes, placed in clusters of floating plants, hatch in about ten days. They are all evidently consistent about the length of time it takes to hatch their eggs, for they all take approximately the same time to develop.

Slightly smaller than *Panchax sexfasciatus* is *Panchax fasciolatus* which is only reported from Sierra Leone. The males of this fish have a spot of red on each scale, and a few bars are visible along the lower body, particularly toward the tail. The females are not spotted, but sport a dark line along the body to the tail. In addition to the bright spots of the body, the male carries red spots on the pale-greenish dorsal, anal and caudal fins. The other fins are the same color but lack the spots. This fish is not well known to aquarists, but is in demand on the few occasions it visits our shores.

A smaller fish from the Congo River is very attractive. This is a bluish animal, with a reddish back and yellow belly. The sides are liberally sprinkled with large bright red spots, and the fins are brilliantly green. These latter are a sure indication of the sex, for the lower part of the tail of the male is considerably lengthened and both the dorsal and tail are tipped with red. The fins of the female are, as usual, small, colorless and round. This two-inch-long fish is called *Panchax microstigma*. It has not been successfully adapted to aquarium life, but since it is sometimes taken in slightly salt water, it is possible that it does not care for the fresh waters of the ordinary aquarium.

The Senegal Panchax, *Panchax senegalensis*, is the last of the West African Panchaxes we include in our category. This is another two-inch fish, almost a complete stranger to American aquaria. If it ever came to this country in any numbers it would, on a basis of color, become immediately popular, for it is a bright gold with about a dozen sloping lines across its body. The unpaired fins—dorsal, tail and anal—are blue, with lines of purple or brown spots across them. The dorsal and anal fins of the males have black edges as well.

All the Panchax are peaceful animals, and eat almost anything in the nature of fish food, although they like a few worm steaks once in a while.

On our way over to India, where there are some more Panchax which are slightly better known than most of the African ones, we shall stop off at Zanzibar or some of the comparatively neighboring Seychelles Islands. These harbor one of the prettiest and most popular of the Panchax. *Panchax playfairi* is of a somewhat heavier build then the West African species and is fairly large, about four inches. While the fish is peaceful, it is sufficiently large to eat some of the smaller fishes commonly kept in community aquaria; for this reason large specimens should be kept with other fish of a comparable size. The color of the animal is predominantly gold, although there is a greenish tint to the sides of the body. There are a number of dotted lines of red running the length of the body, and the fins are very pale brown or yellow. These are also dotted with red. The anal fin of the male is pointed, a sign of sex not really necessary, for the females of this species are barred along the side like the *Panchax chaperi*. So alike are these, indeed, that small specimens of female *playfairi* may easily be mistaken for *chaperi* at a casual glance. The clear dorsal of the female, however, has a dark splotch at its base which is lacking in *chaperi*.

The eggs of these species are large and easily noticed. They hatch in about ten or twelve days, if they are not eaten by the parent fish. The spawning is similar to the others of the genus, and the methods I have described of securing the eggs are practiced by breeders of the animals.

In Madras, India, is another small Panchax, popular when it is obtainable. This, *Panchax parvus*, is about two inches long, but most specimens are smaller and the fish is generally reported to be the smallest of the Panchaxes. It is a very colorful fish. The dark sides are almost purple along the lower edge, and the flanks of the dark brown body are covered with alternate rows of brilliant green, gold and red spots, which run over onto the fins. The body of the female is merely tinged with the bright colors of her mate, and the fins are entirely clear of spots and are a solid color which may shade from a pale to a rich orange.

This species will breed in an aquarium fairly readily, requiring the same general treatment as do the others of its family. In this case, however, the eggs are very small, and are not easily noticed.

From the same waters, and those to the southward, along the Malabar coast comes the Panchax which shares with the Chaperi the greatest popularity. This is a very old favorite of the aquarist and, from almost every standpoint from which the aquarist judges fishes, it is deservedly so. It is colorful, peaceful, hardy and easily bred. The colors in general resemble those of *Panchax parvus*, but as the fish is at least twice as large, they are very much more obvious. The basic color is not quite as dark as *parvus*, and there are more green dots along the side than there are red. However, the fins are distinctly red, although there are a number of bright-yellow, almost gold, spots upon them. There is also a line of yellow and a red edge on the dorsal, caudal and anal fins. All this glory is of the male. The female is just a plain fish silver, which is broken by a few dark bars across the lower part of the body. She does have a little red in the edges of her fins, however.

There need be no doubt whether or not this fish has spawned, for the eggs are enormous compared with those of fishes of a similar size. They are about one-eighth of an inch in diameter, and can be seen very easily. There are lots of them, too, for the fish spawns readily and under a considerable variety of conditions which could be expected to inhibit such activity. The youngsters are hardy, and ready to do their share toward the continuance of the species when they are only three or four months old.

This fish is *Panchax lineatus,* sometimes known as "Rubrostigma." It exhibits a trait which is the exact opposite of that of *Panchax chaperi.* The vast majority of the babies of *lineatus* are males, a condition for which there does not seem to be any reason, unless it is because there is so much breeding that only a few females are required to keep the population stable. Such things are not understood, and open almost unlimited fields for biological investigation. Of course, not everyone can go to India to study such fishes and then trot back to the wilds of Africa to compare notes with those obtained from a study of *chaperi* which has so many females, but considerable ground work could be done in the laboratory, and a firm base to start from could be established. Of course, such traits may be purely domestic ones, and of no incidence in the wild at all, but it is odd that the most prolific of this genus should develop peculiarities under what are manifestly favorable conditions.

There is another fish, a relative, which is distributed pretty nearly all over India and the Malay Peninsula. This fish is *Panchax panchax,* and must have given many headaches to those men who tried to identify and tie a tag to it, for it is extremely variable in color, and at one time there were at least three recognized strains. Latterly, however, two have been given variety names and the fishes captured and examined seem to fit one or the other of the two descriptions. Specimens of a predominantly blue color, or of a shade of green body with a blue lower region, may be encountered. There are different types even reported as coming from the same brood of young, although where such a Mendelian complex came from it is hard to say. In any case, the fish that looks blue has a spot of blue on each scale, and bright yellow fins. The greenish fish has fins of other shades of yellow, even orange, and the blue underside of the body. They are both about three inches long and sometimes will spawn tiny eggs in the aquarium. The fact that they are not so easily spawned in domesticity may be because they are occasionally found in water which is slightly salt, a condition which rarely obtains in aquaria, but may possibly be necessary to the fish. Another problem for someone to try to solve!

The eggs, of course, are left in the masses of floating vegetation and hatch in about two weeks, in conformity with those of the rest of the genus.

## III. Cynolebias

On the opposite side of the world, about Southern Brazil and Uruguay, there are some very odd relatives of the Panchaxes. These are the *Cynolebias,* one or two species of which occasionally bob up in tropical fish stores.

Besides having breeding habits which are somewhat unusual, these fishes also show somewhat unusual differences between the sexes.

One of the methods used in identifying fishes is to count the rays and spines of the fins. These rays and spines are the stiff supports of the membranous part of the fish, and are more or less constant in each species. However, in *Cynolebias* the ray counts for the dorsal and anal fins are not the same in the two sexes. This is of importance to the taxonomist, and interesting to the novice, who, however, does not spend much of his time counting rays or scales. (The number of scales is also used in the identification of fishes, which accounts in part for the fact that even the most expert are sometimes nonplused when asked to identify a living fish, although they can readily name the fish when it is dead.) These Cynolebias live in holes and puddles which occasionally go dry during the dry season. Rivulus are found in the same kinds of places too, but they have not developed any peculiar eggs such as the genus we are talking of. These fishes bury their fairly large eggs in the mud. According to the experience of aquarists who have tried to duplicate conditions for the fishes, the eggs seem to require some sort of cooking before they hatch out. In any case, they take as long as six weeks to hatch, during which time the mud in which they are lying may be almost completely dried. When the water returns in the rainy season, the eggs hatch, and the baby fishes start a new population of Cynolebias. At least, that is what is reported, and as we know that the eggs take about one month to hatch in aquarium conditions, and that they are buried in the mud and that the fishes are taken from muddy little holes which may well dry out before they are filled again by the rains, there may be some truth to the story. Whether or not that is so, the fishes are quite pretty little creatures, those species which have been tried in aquaria living fairly well and adding a dash of color to the tank.

*Cynolebias bellotti* is a dark-blue fish with lines of light-blue dots along the body, if you are looking at a male; brown if you are looking at a female. (The sexes are differently colored as well as having a different fin-ray count.) There is a dark line running through the eye of the male. The fins are blue-gray or blue-green, and the fish is about three inches long. It comes from the La Plata River region.

*Cynolebias adloffi* is a lighter blue and comes from Port Alegre in Brazil. The females are still a brownish color not comparable with their gem-like brothers. The males have the stripe through the eye, like the first one, but they have, in addition, several black lines across the body. There may be ten or twelve of these. The lines are suggested on the body of the female, and are not very distinct. The males of this species have light-blue dots too. The female has a number of brown dots scattered about on her body. This fish is only about two inches long.

From the same general region comes another of the same genus. This, very like *Cynolebias bellotti* in appearance, is about four inches long. However, it may be distinguished by the difference in the arrangement of the dots. In this species, *Cynolebias wolterstorffi*, the dots are scattered all over the fish, and the female is marbled in brown.

There are a few more species of this genus, but since they are almost unheard of as aquarium fishes, we shall not bother with them any more. Instead, we shall go on to their much better-known relatives, the Rivulus.

## IV. Rivulus

The members of this group of fishes are all American, from either South or Central America or the nearby islands. They have the same habit as the Panchaxes and Aphyosemion of hanging fairly motionless in thickets of plants, but they are by no means inert or listless, as they will demonstrate if the cover is left off the aquarium, for they can and will jump surprising distances, and can direct themselves with a great deal of accuracy through even very small holes in the cover. This may be due in part to their habitats, for these fishes, too, live where they are liable to be dried out, and when the water of their pool is evaporated, they hop around considerably, presumably looking for water. They seem to be undistrubed if they do not find any for a while, however, for they can stay out of it for hours. One explorer in Central America reports that the low bushes between water holes were literally covered with Rivulus, probably in transition from one pool to another, for they were all alive and apparently in good health.

The eggs of these species are slow in development, taking about two weeks to hatch. They are, almost without exception, adhesive and are deposited among floating leaves of small clusters of plants.

For many years *Rivulus urophthalmus* was a very popular fish. Aquarists who value good looks and colors still treasure a pair or two of this species, for they are very lovely and are hardy and prolific.

There are two types, the Green which is brownish-green and covered with red dots both on the body and the fins, and the Red, which is really yellow, but the red spots are more evident against the lighter body. The difference between the sexes is peculiar. In the green phase, the female has an ocellus of dark color on the root of the tail. The males do not have this spot. In the red phase, the spot on the female is missing, but she may be distinguished by a lighter color than the male, and the relative paucity of red spots.

It is noteworthy that although this species will usually eat all their eggs if they can get at them, if the fish are left undisturbed in an aquarium for several months, there will always be little ones, but some careful searching must be done to find them. Is it possible that there is some instinct which prompts these unreasoning animals, living as they do now in a complete microcosm, to leave a few eggs to insure the survival of the species.

This fish originated in the Amazon and is about two and a half inches when full grown.

Another Rivulus of the same general appearance as the Green Rivulus in its red phase is *Rivulus xanthonotus*. This fish, from the same regions and of approximately the same size, may be still another color phase of *Rivulus urophthalmus*, for the only discernible difference is that this fish has a dark back and yellow stripes down its body. These, for a fish which shows such distinctly different color patterns as a green body on one type and a yellow body on the other, are hardly definitive enough for a different species, although a sufficient number of the fish are not available for us to be positive either way.

A comparatively recent introduction which has taken a considerable hold on the fancy of aquarists is *Rivulus cylindraceus*. This fish does not seem to share the leaping proclivities of the Amazon species, but otherwise it lives in a similar manner. It also deposits its eggs in the clusters of floating plants, and stays motionless for hours, with just its head showing. The sexes may be distinguished by the spot on the tail of the female. The colors are complicated, but the general impression is that of a fairly dark fish. The body is dark green, with a number of very fine lines of a lighter green, and a number of light green dots toward the head and red dots toward the tail. These lines and dots do not form any definite pattern at all, but give the impression, as the fish moves from light to shadow in the aquarium, that it is changing color. There are a few fixed marks. A dark-red line runs from the head to the tail of the animal, and a metallic blue spot adorns the shoulder. The fins are lustrous green and blue, with white and red margins. As with the Green Rivulus, this fish sometimes will eat the eggs and young. Most fishes will, on occasion, but if some of these fish are left undisturbed, young ones will always be found in the aquarium, always assuming, of course, that there are at least a few cubic inches of matted plants floating about.

This fish is a Cuban, about two inches long, and quite peaceful in the community aquarium.

*Rivulus strigatus*, a tiny fish from the Amazon, is only about one and a half inches long, but what it lacks in length it makes up in color. It is dark blue on the sides, with an almost black back, and yellow-orange lower body. The lower part of the head is a bright, deep yellow. Along the sides are lines of red dots. (Notice that these Rivulus all have dots on their bodies.) Across the sides are a series of red lines. These are not straight down, but, starting at the top at an angle toward the head, change direction halfway down, and then point toward the bottom and tail of the fish—a very curious herring-bone effect. The fins are blue or yellow, with bars over most of them, and with red margins. The female has no red on her fins, and is much less attractive to our eyes. She suits the males, however, for they deposit eggs, which, as is the case with the other Rivulus, do not generally grow into mature fish. There seems to be a catch somewhere about these fish, for even when the eggs, which are not numerous in aquaria, hatch, the young fish just die. Whatever they need for a sturdy growth is very evidently lacking in the average aquarium, but so far no one has discovered what it is. It is a pity, for the fish is very beautiful.

Perhaps, though, if the fish were hardy and bred freely, it would lose its novelty, as so many other beautiful fishes do.

A fish which has lost favor these last few years, but which is quite nice-looking and easily reared in aquaria, is *Rivulus ocellatus*, from São Paulo. This fish is about two and a half inches long and distinctly yellowish. The spots, however, are blue, very dark and conspicuous. These frequently form lines across the body. There is also a spot at the base of the tail which is more distinct on the female. The fins are one or another shade of brown, and are edged with black in the male. The breeding behavior is about characteristic of the genus, and the fish is quite peaceful and a pleasant community aquarium fish.

A slender, rather pretty fish from the Southern States of Mexico is often available in the pet shops. This is *Rivulus tenuis,* about three inches long. The sexes of this species are well defined by color. The females, somewhat variable, are a shade of brown with a few darker spots on the side and a large tail spot. The males are quite bright, with a dark back, shading to a blue ventral region. This, with the part of the head below the eyes, is spotted with red, and the lips are red too. The fins are yellow, with red lines and dots, and the tail fin has a black edge.

The eggs of *Rivulus tennuis* are of the usual type of the genus. They are adhesive and are deposited among clusters of floating plants, where they take about two weeks to hatch.

From Colombia, toward the mouth of the River Magdalena, comes another little fish which is known to aquarists as *Rivulus brevis,* or the Short Rivulus, which is not a Rivulus at all, although it is of a similar appearance. The breeding behavior is most un-Rivulus-like for the eggs instead of being attached to vegetation are buried in the dirt and sand at the bottom of the water. *Rachovia brevis* has a lovely mixture of colors. Each scale has a violet edge which is quite apparent against the general body color of blue or green, or rather a blend of both these colors. The fins, except the tail, are iridescent, sometimes violet, sometimes blue, sometimes green. The tail, of which the upper and lower rays are produced, is gray, speckled with blue dots. The lower rays of the tail are pink or dark yellow. A most attractive ensemble. As might be expected, these lovely colors are only found in their entirety in the male; the female is of a much less vivid splendor, although she is not at all colorless. Both sexes are about the same size, averaging less than two inches.

Perhaps owing to their habitat, which is slightly off the most frequented lanes of traffic, this species is not a regular aquarium fish, although it does well under suitable conditions not impossible to maintain in domestic aquaria. It is quite peaceful and well worth an effort to procure and keep.

## V. Medaka

From Japan—we have not listed any fish from Japan before —comes a little fish which is sporadic in its appeal to the aquarist, although it is not particularly beautiful. It is not strictly a "tropical fish," for its native waters are not torrid in temperature, as are the waters of many of the usual "tropicals." In fact, this fish has been turned loose in our own country in parts of California, where it is reported to be thriving. This coolish water origin does not interfere with its ability to live in the warm waters of domestic aquaria, and while it will not breed as freely as our friend the Guppy, it does breed and reproduce its kind fairly readily.

This is the Japanese Medaka, *Oryzias latipes*. The original color of this species is brown—a sort of silvery brown like an old piece of furniture with a patina reflecting from it. It is, however, subject to considerable variation in aquaria, and possibly in the wild, and has been the source of considerable genetical knowledge by reason of these different color phases. The usual type sold in stores is light yellow in color, but this same type will produce young which show different shades of yellow, some as deep as orange. There are other distinctly colored fish. Some are red; others a sort of mottled red; some blue ones turn up; some are white; and there is a mottled white strain. In all colors, it is the same fish, with the same habits of breeding, the same sexual characteristics and of approximately the same size.

The breeding is somewhat unusual. The female liberates eggs which are adhesive, and which sometimes remain attached to the body or fins, or both, of the fish for several days. They hang down at the ends of tiny strings of mucus or a similar substance, and seem to be firmly attached. However, as she swims about the tank, the eggs, at the end of their strings, are brushed off the fish and onto the leaves of plants, where they hang like little lanterns, each on its own string. Whether the fish is supposed to carry the eggs, and brushing off by the plants is accidental, or whether she intends the eggs to be attached to plants—or whether the whole business has no definite purpose or plan behind it—no one knows, nor is there much chance that it will be found out, but there the eggs are, suspended by the short stalks from leaves in the aquarium. Those that are not eaten hatch in about two weeks or less, depending on the conditions of heat and light in the aquarium.

Both sexes are about the same size—one and a half inches long, and both are similarly colored, but there is one very distinct mark of sex which is easily recognized. The rays in the dorsal fin of the female are all the same distance apart. In the male, all but the last ray are evenly spaced. The last ray is about twice as far from its nearest neighbor as any of the others. This is a small characteristic, but once it is known, it may be easily noticed.

These little fish are quite peacefully disposed, and fit into the general scheme of the community aquarium nicely, but they are usually neglected for the more colorful or larger species of aquarium fishes, although they are pretty enough, and of sufficient interest to warrant a small aquarium to themselves.

The Medaka were at one time placed, with similar fishes of India and the Celebes, in the genus Aplocheilus, but neither the Indian nor the Celebean Medaka are in the slightest degree popular aquarium fishes, nor have they the same variety of color that the Nipponese Medaka sports; so we shall not bother with them.

## VI. The Lebias

From our own eastern coasts, the coasts of Northern Africa, Asia Minor, the Red Sea and adjacent waters, and the fresh waters of the lands about the Mediterranean—Palestine, Syria, along the southern shore of that inland sea to Algeria, and the northern portion touching Italy and Spain—and even as far east as Northern India, through Persia—comes a pretty genus of fishes commonly known as the Lebias, a carry-over of their former generic name *Lebias*. (We mentioned their relative, *Cynolebias*, some fishes ago.) None of the species from salt or near-salt water is really suitable for ordinary aquaria, although they may be gradually turned over into fresh-water fishes. This turning is somewhat drastic, necessitating considerable adjustment by the fishes, which is sometimes too much for them, and they die. However, they may be kept in cool water in which there is a small quantity of salt, and will well repay the effort entailed in the color they show.

The Sheepshead Lebia, *Cyprinodon variegatus*, is the American representative of the genus, and is a truly beautiful fish.

Over the steel-blue sides of the males are scattered spots of a more intense blue, while the lower part of the body is a deep yellow or orange. The females are not so brightly colored, and they have a number of dark narrow bars across the body. Not much attention is paid to the heavy, adhesive eggs which are spawned in groups of a few at a time. These sink in the water until they find something solid to stick to, where they hatch in about a week or so. When the babies are still less than half an inch long, they bear the characters and colors of their parents, although they are not full grown until they are about one year old. Three inches appears to be the maximum length. This local fish does not appear frequently in stores, perhaps because it is hard to keep, or because it is too near to us to be valued. In any case, this is a loss to aquatic endeavors, for it is as lovely as many more exotic specimens and of no particularly greater difficulty to maintain.

Two related species of Lebias are more diverse in origin, coming from both the semi-fresh and the salt waters of quite a large slice of the world, bounded by a line drawn southward from Italy to Tunisia and Libia, eastward through Egypt, Arabia and Persia to Baluchistan, probably north into Afghanistan, westward through Persia again, and across the ancient lands of the Eastern Mediterranean back to Italy. Both of these fishes are attractively marked, but neither is popular in aquaria, although they may be more easily adapted to the fresh water and high temperature of the ordinary aquarium than many other fishes about which aquarists become exercised.

Related to these is *Cyprinodon iberus,* the Spanish Lebia. This one, a blue-backed fish with a yellow ventral section, is about two inches long, from Spain and Algeria. It is entirely a fresh-water fish, and, as usual, the female is not nearly as bright as the male. An additional difference between males and females is that the former has a series of dark lines across his body and the latter has only brown spots. These fish deposit adhesive eggs about the leaves of plants, and the young break loose after about ten days.

There are a number of Fundulus in this family, of which a few are suitable aquarium fishes, but none of which is really in much demand. The Golden Killifish, *Fundulus chrysotus,* from the marshlands of our Southeastern States is in periodic demand, probably because it is the prettiest of the genus. It is a chunky fish about three inches long, with blue-green sides covered with bright red spots which reflect golden glints, as suggested in the name "chrysotus," as the fish swims about. The fins also carry these spots. The female, browner in the body, is spotted with silver, and there are no marks on her fins. As with many others of the family of Cyprinodonts, this fish deposits its eggs in clusters of floating leaves, where they hatch in about two weeks.

A more southerly neighbor of the Golden Killifish comes from Florida, and is also fairly well known to aquarists. This, unlike the last, is somewhat pugnacious, and is not suitable for inclusion in a community aquarium. It is, however, a lovely little fish of about three inches, brightly colored with lines of steel blue dots which run down each row of scales, and half a dozen or so gold or green intermediate stripes. Its name, American Flag Fish, comes from a remote resemblance to the United States' colors, and the very large dorsal fin, which could be imagined to resemble a flag. As is to be expected, the female is much more demure in coloration, light brown sides with splotches of darker brown irregularly placed, and a dark spot toward the end of the dorsal fin completing her decoration. This dorsal spot is also present on the fin of the male, but is not nearly as evident.

Unlike most of its relatives, this fellow builds a nest, or rather sketchily excavates and cleans a shallow depression in the sand or gravel at the bottom of the water for the reception of the eggs which he sometimes attends and sometimes neglects. In any case, the young hatch in about four or five days. Whether the male looks after the eggs or young, or not, he will not usually bother them, nor will he fight with the female, unless the tank in which they are living is too small and they are thrown too closely together; in which case, of course, any fish which has any fight in him will show it. The scientific name of the American Flag Fish is *Jordanella floridæ*. It is the last of this very well-scattered family of fishes that come under our consideration in this group.

# Chapter 11

## Miscellaneous Fishes

THERE ARE a number of other aquarium fishes, each in its own way suitable to the conditions of domestic aquaria, but there are no more families that contain many suitable species like the preceding groups. Many of the families are represented by only one species, while a few of them include two or three fishes that fit all the requirements of pet fish.

## I. Nandids

One of these families is the Nandidæ, species of which occur about the Indian peninsula, tropical Africa and South America. Most of the aquarium species are small, deep-bodied animals resembling miniature Sun-fishes.

One representative of this family comes from the countries half way along the northern shores of South America, and is looked upon as something of a novelty. This is the Casarab, *Polycentrus schomburgki*. Specimens have been imported more or less frequently into the United States, but the fish, while it will breed in aquaria, does not become particularly well known. There is not a great deal of difference in size—about two inches long—or in coloration between males and females. Either may be light brown or quite black, or any of the shades between, but as a general rule, the female is a little lighter than her brother. When the color is light, a number of blue spots are visible along the sides of both sexes, but these disappear as the fish darkens. The fins are transparent, and almost invisible, giving the fish a curious appearance. The Casarab, like all its relatives, is not a very active fish, much more content in a dark hole where it can lie undisturbed than in a clear aquarium with light sand and plants, and no rocks. The eggs are spawned in cave-like structures, if any are available, and are usually attached to the overhanging roof. If there is nothing else, the inside of a flower-pot lying on its side will be used, after it has been carefully cleaned by the male, although

139

these fish seem happier if a few very dark or black rocks are built in to the aquarium, leaving plenty of murky crevices between the pieces. After the eggs are deposited, the male will take care of them, and of the young after they hatch, which they do in about four days. Since neither the males nor the females are given to fighting, any effort to defend the young is usually unnecessary in the well-managed aquarium. Perhaps it is because of their lethargic habits that they are so neglected by enthusiastic aquarists, for the incubation of the eggs is no less interesting than with many other popular fishes, and their colors no less beautiful.

Of a similar shape, but lighter color, and perhaps half an inch longer than the Casarab, is *Badis badis* of India. This species is always available, and is bred fairly easily in aquaria to meet a discriminating demand. The Badis is given to fighting and is not safely mixed with smaller fishes, or with fishes of an equal size, and when eggs or young are being cared for by the male, the female must not be allowed near him. The colors of this species are varied from a light green to black, although the fish usually reserve the black color for the breeding period. When the fish is in the light-color phases, a blue shoulder spot is visible, and sometimes a number of dark lines across the body are in evidence too. These latter are not to be relied upon, however, for the fish will, more likely than not, be of one color. There is no sexual difference in color usually; sometimes the female is lighter than the male, although not always, but there is a definite distinguishing mark in the shape of the dorsal fin, which is pointed in the male and round in the female.

This species deposits its eggs in small shallow depressions in sand which it digs for itself, and the eggs are attended closely by the male. Like the Labyrinth Fishes, there is an embrace between the sexes when the eggs are released, and like them, the female goes about her business while the male takes over the care of the eggs and the youngsters for a week or so. (The eggs hatch in about three days and the babies, when they are about four days old, are driven from home.) Unlike the Labyrinth Fishes, however, the male will sometimes court another female, if one is available, and place her eggs in the same nest he used at first. He does not seem to mind whether the first female comes back or whether others come over. He will mate with them, look after any eggs that result and then start all over again. This may go on for a month or two, but if the tank is small, there will soon be no fishes, for they will fight, as I said before, and while the weaker ones will be killed, the stronger ones will frequently die of the wounds inflicted in the marital battles.

These fish like dark holes to hide in, although they do not seem to mind open water nearly as much as the Casarabs.

There is a Nandid which is occasionally brought here from the Niger region of Africa. This, *Polycentropsis abbreviata,* is about three inches long, or perhaps a little longer, and is similar to the Casarab in a general way. It is something of the same shape, and the fins are almost completely transparent, and the colors are similar to the lighter phases of the South American fish. There is a considerable difference in the breeding habits, however, which are reported to be similar to those of the Labyrinth Fishes. A hundred, more or less, eggs are thrust into a raft of bubbles made by the fish, where they hatch in about six days. While this fish is scarce in aquaria, and there is not a great deal known of its aquarium habits, it is worth mentioning if only because it repeats that remarkable nesting habit, and since this fish has no auxiliary breathing mechanism, some of our ideas about the necessity of air for the baby Paradise and Fighting Fishes may have to be modified.

The Leaf Fish, *Monocirrhus polyacanthus,* is another South American Nandid. Its common name is derived from its dead-leaf-like appearance, although it is sometimes called the Bearded Nandid, from the small tab of flesh which sticks out from its chin. This, indeed, increases the fish's resemblance to a leaf, for it looks for all the world like the stalk of a leaf. The color of the fish is a tan-gold, over which are a number of irregular dark blotches. Both sexes are alike, and they are almost impossible to distinguish. In fact, it is impossible to separate the male from the female, except when they are breeding. Then, by the shape of the ovipositor, the sexes may be differentiated.

This fish, from the leaf-covered small streams of the Amazon drainage, has a peculiar habit of drifting about, head down and tail up, among the dead floating leaves among which it lives. When a small fish, deceived by the stillness of the leaves, ventures within an inch or two of the stalk of this particular leaf, the whole end of the leaf opens, and the little fish is no more!

To say that the fish drifts is not quite correct, for it has all its movements under control, but it certainly gives that impression as it moves sideways and up and down the aquarium without a perceptible motion of its fins. However, close observation reveals that parts of the dorsal and anal and all of the pectoral fins are quite transparent, and are in constant motion; and by the size and speed of the floating débris set in motion by these invisible fins, they can cause quite a powerful current.

A maximum size of about three and a half inches is reached by these fishes, but they breed when they are about two inches long. The eggs are adhesive and are attached to the floating leaves of surface plants, when the fish has any choice. When it has none, the eggs will be attached to the lower surface of leaves lying horizontally in the aquarium. They hatch in about three days, and the young are free—swimming in about two days more. About one hundred eggs seem to be a fair expectation, and the mass of eggs is attended by one of the parents, which treats the other with the utmost ferocity if it draws too near to the nest. Which fish attends the nest is difficult to say, for there is, as I have said before, the most remarkable similarity between the sexes. One of the collectors of such fish is of the opinion that it is the female that looks after the eggs. He may be right, but if so, this species differs from the other members of the family, in which it is the male that swims guard. Whichever it is, it is quite essential that the other be either removed from the tank, or the tank be large enough for it to get out of reach of the guarding fish, which chases it to the farthest corner away from the nest and will not allow it to move from there. This is one sure way of courting trouble, for if the fish cannot get out of its corner to eat, it will, in hunger, go after anything within range, and a battle-royal may be the outcome, from which neither of the parent fish, nor any of the young, may emerge in one piece. This fish is *not* a community fish, for it will only eat living fish, and several large Guppies seem to stimulate its appetite for other, larger fishes, as big as two-inch Swordtails.

There are one or two other Nandids which are quite rare, so rare that there is no need to mention them by name.

## II. The Glass Fish

One family of generally salt-water fishes sends a very popular fresh-water species to our tanks. This is the family Chandidæ of both the Indian and Pacific Oceans. Any fresh-water fishes of the family are in reality from brackish water, but they can adjust themselves very nicely to fresh water, and are reported to breed sometimes up rivers far beyond the reach of tidal water. The one species which arrives in our tanks is the Glass Fish, which is taken in the waters of Bengal and Baluchistan. The most usual name of this fish is *Ambassis lala,* from the local Indian name, but this has been changed to *Ambassis ranga,* a technical change which does not interest the aquarist very much.

It is a small, deep-bodied fish of about two inches or less, and almost half that high. It is very thin, and while the color is slightly yellow or golden, it is so thin and the tissues are so colorless that it is almost transparent. Parts of the internal machinery of the animal may be clearly seen, even to the beating of the heart, although the most noticeable organ is the swimbladder, which shines like a drop of silver. The backbone and ribs are also in plain sight, and a photograph looks like an X-ray picture. The sexes are very difficult to distinguish. In fact, they are almost impossible to pick, for while there is a slight difference in the depth of the blue at the edge of the dorsal fin, the color is so delicate that it is almost impossible to see in either sex. While it is unusual to have these fish spawning in aquaria, they have done so. The eggs, very small and adhesive, are deposited in the fine matted leaves of floating plants where they hatch the same day, in about twelve hours. Young specimens have three dark lines across the body, and are even higher in the body in proportion to their length than are their parents, but few young Glass Fish born in tanks survive more than a few days. The fish available in the stores are almost invariably imported, usually from Germany, where they are apparently bred with a good deal more success than we have with them here. Whether this is due to the natural conditions obtaining in parts of Europe, we do not know, but we do know that many fishes which never spawn on this side of the Atlantic appear to be bred regularly on the other. Natural conditions are probably more suitable there, for fish fanciers from Europe who have been able to produce large numbers of the rarer fishes at home never seem to be able to do it here.

Be that as it may, the Glass Fish, which has to be imported, is very popular here, and is quite suitable for the community tank, living in perfect amity with other fishes from all parts of the world.

*Ambassis commersoni,* another Glass Fish somewhat longer than *Ambassis lala,* sometimes arrives here from Africa. While this species probably spends a good deal of its time in fresh water, specimens have been caught in salt water from the decks of steamers, and have been transported without trouble to New York where they have been kept in regular ocean water as well as in domestic fresh-water aquaria. We have no records of the spawning behavior.

## III. Gobies

A family which sends us a few specimens occasionally is that of the Gobiidæ. This family is very large and of world-wide distribution, but occurs mostly in tropical sea waters. They are generally inactive beasts, some suitable for aquarium uses are even called "Sleepers." Usually they are tough, in both interpretations of the word, for they will eat almost anything they can get their mouths around, and they will tolerate all sorts of conditions which would destroy almost any other fish. Some of the species have been reported to have auxiliary breathing organs, sometimes located in the skin, but this is only theoretical, nothing being very definitely known about it. We do know that the Sleepers will live for months under almost anaërobic conditions, seemingly without distress, and one, the most popular of all of them, spends more than half his life out of water entirely, hopping about with exceeding agility after winged insects, of which he can catch enough to support him very nicely.

This is the famous Mudspringer, *Periophthalmus kœlreuteri*. At home on the shores of tropical seas all over the world except South America, this fish is taken most frequently on the mud flats of the estuaries of large rivers, where the water is at least brackish. Whether it is, or is entirely fresh, or entirely salt, seems to be a matter of supreme indifference to it, however, for it lives for years in either one or the other. Its diet seems to bother it little too, for small marine crustaceans, large earthworms, fresh-water worms or terrestrial insects are all taken with equal relish and considerable activity. While the fish swims well, some of its fins are adapted for terrestrial locomotion. The pectoral fins grow at the end of a short, stout stalk, and are articulated like a wrist. The fin proper is very large, and splays out when it is rested against a hard surface. The rays are fairly stiff, for when the animal wishes to raise himself, he can do so on the ends of the rays, much as we stand on our toes to look over a high object. In addition to these fins being specially adapted, the ventral fins have short stalks which are joined together for a part of their length. These fins, while not so strongly developed as the pectorals, are quite strong, and when the fish is resting out of the water, it frequently sits on a tripod formed by the two ventral fins and the tail and folds the two pectoral fins along its sides, much as a bird folds its wings when it is sitting or standing on a bough.

The colors are not bright, until one looks closely, when lines and dots of brilliant metallic blue may be seen all over the brownish body and on the back fins. There are two dorsal fins on all Gobies. The structure of the body is peculiar. The head is very large, and the animal tapers off to a slender tail. On top of the sides of the rather squarish head are the eyes, large and protruding. These can turn in their sockets considerably, and they can be, and often are, "popped," a proceeding which is exceedingly strange to watch and which seems to fulfil the same duty as our lids do when we blink our eyes.

These fishes seem to be particularly fond of mosquitoes; at least, they are most frequently found where there are swarms of those little pests, and, although there are lots of fish about the mud, they are so agile that they are almost impossible to catch without a net. They are supposed to hide in crab holes along the edge of the water, but after watching their activity in an aquarium, I am of the opinion that the supposed crab holes are of their own digging, for they have an insatiable desire to dig, and spend a great deal of effort digging holes, carrying the sand or mud away in their mouths. After which, they sit for a while in the hole, and then start digging another.

One fish which was quite a pet, jumping up into a hand that was stretched out to it, regularly carried about twenty pounds of sand over a low stone wall, placed there to keep his sand from filling up his swimming hole. On one occasion he moved all the sand over the wall during one night, but he usually moved about half of it, until both sides of the wall had equal amounts of sand and water, and then divided his efforts, sometimes digging on one side and sometimes on the other.

*Periophthalmus* does not usually grow longer than about six inches, and we have no idea of the spawning activity. There is a relative, *Boleophthalmus,* from the most southeasterly regions of Asia which has apparently the same habits.

The Mudspringer, because of its habits of sitting with its head out on the shore and its tail trailing in the water, is supposed to have some sort of dermal respiration, particularly about the tail, a supposition which may well be founded on fact. It also had pads of spongy tissue under the skin of the cheeks, in which it may carry enough water to last it for an hour or so. At one time it was supposed to have a cavity in the head in which water was carried, but those few specimens examined did not include such a reservoir in their internal economy. Whether or not there is any absorption through the skin, the fish which have died in our tanks—they do die, even in the hands of the most experienced aquarists—have always been found lying on their sides, with their heads out of the water and their tails in, much as if they were lying in a bed with their weary heads on a pillow. This may be merely coincidence, but it may be that the fish in its extremity placed itself in the position which was most comfortable and entailed the least drain on its vitality.

Of not nearly so interesting habits are the Sleepers. These

occur on both sides of the strip of land which connects North and South America. On one side, the Atlantic Sleeper, or Atlantic Sleeping Goby, and on the other, the Pacific Sleeper, or Sleeping Goby, whichever you prefer. There is so little difference externally between these species that it is almost impossible to say which is which, but since they are so alike, it does not matter much to the aquarist. These fishes thrive in an aquarium, growing so big that they become a nuisance, for they will eat anything within reach. Wild specimens are a foot long; the aquarium specimens, which are just babies of an inch or two when they are brought in for our tanks, rarely reaching above six inches. They are quite pretty—an attractive shade of light brown, or tan, with lines of blue and green across the body. They are found in all sorts of water—filthy stagnant fresh water, sweet clear fresh water, brackish or plain salt water, and, as an evidence of their hardiness, they have been caught in the sea on a hook, left on a small boat in the sun for several hours, and then dumped into a fresh-water aquarium without any apparent distress. They hardly ever die in aquaria, seemingly living forever and ever. The harassed aquarist always has a few which never seem to stop growing in his tanks and which he hesitates to throw out. They will uproot plants and destroy smaller fishes with the utmost abandon. They should not be acquired without some little thought for the amount of space they will occupy.

The names and range of the respective species are the Atlantic, *Dormitator maculatus,* which is found along the coasts of the Americas all the way from South Carolina to Brazil, taking in the West Indian Islands on the way, and the Pacific, *Dormitator latifrons,* which has approximately the same long range on the other sides of the continents, from California to Equador. There is no sexual dimorphism.

An Australian cousin of theirs which occasionally comes our way is very interesting and pretty. This is *Mogurnda adspersus,* much easier remembered as the Purple-striped Gudgeon. It is about six inches long when caught wild and full grown, but in aquaria it is mature when smaller and is quite brilliantly marked with purple lines down its side. Both sexes are alike, but the male is the most brightly colored. The breeding is interesting. The eggs are attached to rocks in a jelly-like mass, where they are guarded by the males for about nine days, when they hatch.

Once in a while *Eleotris* are available. They are rather slender fish of silver or silvery brown, with a dark line, which is sometimes broken, running the length of the body. The smallest comes from the east coast of Africa, and is the rarest, but an American species, *Eleotris pisonis,* is fairly common in the stores that deal in such animals. This one grows to a foot or so in length, and is then not a pleasant customer to place with other fishes, for it will heartily eat other smaller ones. Smaller specimens are quite attractive in an aquarium, however, although they are not very active. Like the Sleepers, these fishes do not seem to be in the least particular about the water they live in, for they have been taken from salt water and from the clearest of fresh-water springs.

## IV. Gymnotids

Everybody has heard, although he may not always believe what he hears, of electric fishes. There are such fishes—fishes which can discharge an electric shock powerful enough to paralyze enemies, such as fish-catching men, or their own food. Then the food may be caught without much chasing. The Electric Eel, *Electrophorus electricus* of the Amazon (we have not yet exhausted the possibilities of that strange river) and the rivers north as far as the Orinoco, is one of them. This strange beast, eel-like in shape, can discharge electricity in sufficient quantity to stun such animals as mules, although the eel does not have to touch the mule. Observers have recorded that a shock will last as long as thirty seconds, and that they are unable to move while it is passing through their body. The after effects last for several hours, and are very painful. However, the Electric Eel is a large beast, and is not suitable for ordinary aquaria, unless the tanks are about ten feet long, and broad in proportion. This being out of the question in ordinary domestic economy, we shall have to talk of their smaller relatives, of which a couple do reach our aquaria. Only the smaller specimens are suitable. In fact, the specimens which are brought here are mere babies two or three inches long, but under suitable conditions they will grow to a length of eight or ten inches. These, while they are the same general shape as the Electric Eels, do not discharge any shocks. But they need not be refused a place in the aquarium on that account. They are very graceful creatures with long, slender bodies, which they keep more or less straight when they swim. The locomotor machinery is in the very long anal fin, which stretches in an unbroken line from just behind the head to the tail. This, by the continuous waves running the length of it, pushes them through the water, and they can go backward or forward with equal facility. When they choose, they probably can swim by continuous waves of the body too, but those under observation usually only move the fin when they want to go from here to there. One of the species, *Eigenmannia virescens,* has a large range, including almost all the waterways between Southern Panama and the River Plata. This is equipped with some of the electric organs of the large Electrophorus, but they are apparently shorted somewhere, for they do not seem to work. This beast is a slaty gray, or green, with a number of dark thin lines running the length of the body, but the color seems to vary with the locality from which it comes. Some specimens are red, and because they seem to be able to change their color too, it is pretty hopeless to try to pin them down to one definite color. This fish, under the name "Loga Loga," is considered particularly suitable for food by the natives of British Guiana.

Another species of this family (they are all Gymnotidæ) is *Gymnotus carapo.* This too is often brought in by collectors, although the specimens are usually infants of two or three inches. Like *virescens,* they will live and grow to about six or eight inches in domestic aquaria, and the electric organs are entirely missing. At least, they have not been located. These swim like their relatives, and are very beautifully marked with a series of fine wavy lines diagonally across the body. This one's mouth is slightly undershot, and as it is equipped with a fearsome array of teeth, a head-on view is rather awe-inspiring.

However, all the wild fishes of these two species examined showed a preponderance of insect remains in their stomachs, so we do not have to be nervous lest pet fishes should suddenly take a notion that they would like a meal of fish. It is only when they grow big that they eat other fishes, and as this is an occurrence of exceeding remoteness in aquaria, we do not have to worry about it. Specimens, still going strong, have lived for about two years on chopped-up clams or Tubifex worms; so insects, while they form the major part of the fish's diet in a state of nature, are not an indispensable necessity. *Gymnotus carapo* comes from almost all of the countries bounded by the Atlantic Ocean and the Caribbean Sea on the east and north, and the Andes on the west.

One or two of either of these two smaller species will add considerable novelty and grace to a community aquarium, although they cannot be said to be particularly active. They can dart about with surprising rapidity when the spirit moves them, and they are not especially delicate.

We do not know anything of the spawning behavior of these creatures, although it has been surmised, from a number of indefinite characteristics, too tedious to go into here, that some, if not all, of them are "mouth-breeders." It would be very interesting to find out, but no one has ever reported any spawning activity.

## V. The Catfishes

A large group of fishes, the members of which are increasing in popularity almost daily, is the Catfishes. These are used as scavengers in the community aquarium, although many of the species are beautiful and deserve recognition for other than purely utilitarian virtues.

Technically, the species with which we shall deal in a few words are divided into several groups of which the Naked Cats, the Armored Cats and the Mailed Cats are best known. There is another group of Catfishes which have very unpleasant parasitic habits, of which the less said the better. Anyway, there is only one species of this latter group which ever seems to be brought into this country, and as they always dig into whatever covers the bottom of the tank, and remain invisible all day, only coming out to feed during the dark of the night, one could easily have a tankful of these creatures and label it "Invisible

Fish" and be quite right. For this reason, then, besides their comparative rarity, we shall not say more.

The best known to aquarists of these various families and species are one or two of the genus *Corydoras*. These are sold without much discrimination, as South American Catfish, and are especially recommended for the cleaning department of the aquarium, for they are everlastingly busy chewing up everything they find in the bottom of the tank, reducing what they cannot use as food to fine powder, which is beneficial, if there is not too much of it, for the plants. They do not uproot plants, but will eat all the dead leaves, as well as any dead fish or bits of food. The two particular species of this genus are *Corydoras paleatus* and *Corydoras nattereri*.

The first of these is a really pretty beast of a pleasing shade of light brown, mottled all over with irregularly shaped splotches of black or dark brown. They are not very large, about three inches long, and the head is the biggest part of them, for they taper off both sideways and from top to bottom toward the tail in a fairly regular manner. The dorsal fin is prominent, and nicely marked with bluish or greenish reflections. This fin, with the ventral fins, is pointed in the male, round at the end in the female.

Very few of them seem to be bred in aquaria, and the stories of their breeding activities vary considerably. Creditable eyewitnesses have reported that the female deposits one egg in the center of round-shaped leaves, refusing to spawn if leaves of the proper shape are not provided. Other just as creditable eye-witnesses assert that the female scatters the eggs all over the aquarium until there are several hundred lying about the bottom of the tank. The most generally accepted account of the breeding is that the eggs are released into a pocket formed by the folded ventral fins of the female, where they are fertilized by the male, and then scattered about the tank, where their adhesive quality causes them to stick to the leaves of the plants. The eggs, according to the same series of creditable eyewitnesses, hatch in from two to ten days. I have never seen any of these fish spawning, although there have been many about the New York Aquarium for years, in apparent good health and spirits, so I cannot go on record as to the actual method. This fish comes from the waters of the River Plata and the nearby countries.

*Corydoras nattereri* comes from slightly east and north of *Corydoras paleatus,* and is not as attractive as that fish. It is done in various shades of brown, with a blue sheen. There is a dark line from the gills to the tail and a dark spot beneath and just in front of the dorsal fin. This has the same habits as *Corydoras paleatus,* and the same quality of fish stories are built up about its breeding habits.

Both of these fishes belong to the Armored Catfishes, the Callichthyidæ. The "armor" is a series of hard, bony plates on each side of the body. They are hardy, withstanding the ill-effects of very bad water and, by their activity in breaking down all rotting proteins, improve it. Bad water apparently causes them no distress, and they are quite harmless to other animals. They will, of course, eat any eggs they may find in their wanderings about the tank, so they should never be left in a breeding tank.

The Mailed Catfishes, the Loricariidæ, are represented in the aquarium by one or two of the Plecostomus species. These, too, when they are fairly large, are used as food by the humans of their native haunts, which are spread from Panama as far south as the Argentine. All of these fishes are practically covered with bony plates instead of scales. They are native to fast streams, but they are not very active. This anomaly is because of the curious mouth, which is located under the head, and which is a "sucker" of considerable power. With this, it can head into a strong current and, attached to a stone or other fixed surface, let the rest of the world go by.

*Plecostomus commersoni* seems to be the most popular member of the group.

Because of their sucking mouths and omnivorous habits they are excellent fish to keep in an aquarium, for they hang for hours on the glass walls of the tank, and suck off all the tiny green algæ which grow on it. They have similar scavenging habits to the Corydoras, and are useful in that respect. They are not very pretty, though, and when they hang on the glass and expose their mouth parts, they are repulsive. They are a brownish green in color and have dark marks spread about their bodies. They originate in the streams of Southeastern Brazil.

*Loricaria uracantha* is another of the family. This species shows up occasionally in the pet stores. This fish seems to be particularly hardy, for, although it comes from fast fresh water, it does not seem to mind being kept in the stagnant waters of domestic aquaria at all. Specimens of this species have lived in perfect health in one or another tank in my care for seven or eight years. They do not grow very big in aquaria though, for these same fishes, which must be adults, are not more than about five inches long, although they are recorded as reaching ten or so in the wild.

*Loricaria uracantha* is slightly thinner in build than *Plecostomus,* and is dark in color, almost black sometimes, but it is possible that they change their color to suit their environment. They have the same habits of chewing up everything chewable they find lying about the tank, and will speedily reduce any dead vegetation or other débris to a fine powder—sediment I suppose it should be called—which will cloud the tank at the slightest disturbance.

As with other Catfish, no definite information regarding the breeding behavior is available. Something else for the biologist or aquarist to work on!

A very tiny relative of these fishes comes from Brazil. This is *Otocinclus vittatus,* a beautiful little fellow of not more than one and a half inches long. Like its larger relatives, it has the bony plates and sucking mouth of the family. It is tan in color, with black or dark-brown marks scattered over its sides, and it carries a very obvious dorsal fin. While this little fish will suspend itself for hours from the glass of the aquarium, its small size also enables it to cling to the slender leaves of such plants as Vallisneria. These it cleans of algæ, much as its larger relatives do the glass. It also rests on leaves of Vallisneria without using its mouth. It holds its fairly well-developed ventral fins downward and inward, one on either edge of the leaf, and just "sits" for hours.

*Otocinclus arnoldi,* a fish of similar size and habits, has a stripe down its body. These little fishes are very attractive, but they are so small that they are not always in evidence.

A very curious-looking fish once in a while wanders into the nets of the collectors. This is another Catfish of a different family. From its appearance, an imaginative aquarist called it the "Frying-pan Catfish," and he was about right too, for the whole family are broad, flat fishes with fairly long tails sticking out from behind their roundish bodies. The one of the family (Aspredinidæ) generally brought in is *Bunocephalus gronovii*, from the most easterly section of South America. While this fish is quite hardy, and though small, safe from the attacks of fishes not large enough to swallow it whole, it does not achieve a great popularity because, first, it is not available more than once or twice a year, when the large collections of fishes come from South America, and second, because it burrows under the surface of the sand in the aquarium and almost always stays out of sight. As an instance, three of these fishes were placed in a nice clean tank when they were about two inches long. They were not seen again for almost two years. Then the tank was taken down, and, as the sand was being cleaned, they appeared, healthy and strong about three and a half inches long! In all that time, they had never been in evidence, although they had gotten about the tank enough to get sufficient food almost to double their original size. The maximum length reported is about six inches, and nothing of their sexual characteristics or breeding habits is known. As an instance of the toughness of their bony exterior and of their ability to hide away, specimens have lived for months with hungry and predatory Piranhas without coming to harm. This instance, however, may be adduced as an example of the lack of aggressiveness of those same Piranhas; so you can please yourselves as to which is right.

When we have said something about the Naked Catfishes, the family Siluridæ, we shall leave this whole group.

These Naked Cats are spread widely over the world. Some few of them are taken in salt water, but the vast majority are fresh-water species, coming from the streams and ponds of both the Americas and of Europe, Asia and Africa. They are strange animals. None of them has scales and some of them swim about on their backs! One species, the Gaff-topsail Catfish of the sea, is a mouth-breeder, carrying its eggs and young about in that safe respository. Another discharges electricity at anything it does not like or would like to eat.

However, there are not many of them which meet all the conditions necessary to life in a small aquarium; so in spite of all the novelties of which we could boast if we had a full collection of this family, we shall have to be content with those few that can adapt themselves to the rather unnatural conditions of the domestic aquarium.

One of these is *Pimelodella gracilis*, a fish fairly wide-spread in its habitat, which extends from the Plata to the Orinoco. This fellow is a light tan in color—almost pale yellow—but here again we encounter the ability of fishes to change their colors, for against a dark background, the fish will appear to be a dark green. In whatever color phase he happens to be observed, he has the appearance of translucency and delicacy. He is slender in build, and has long whiskers. The spines of his dorsal fin may or may not be poisonous. Opinions differ, and I have not attempted to find out. He is, however, a useful scavenger, scouting about the bottom of the tank in search of overlooked bits of food which he seizes avidly and swallows with amazing rapidity. Pieces of meat half as big as his body disappear almost the instant his mouth finds them. Ordinarily lying still about the tank, he becomes exceedingly active when there is any possibility of food; then he chases about, his whiskers waving wildly as he flashes back and forth in search of the food he smells. If he doesn't smell the food, I don't know how he discovers it in the tank, for he always comes to life when a bit of food is dropped anywhere within the water, although he may have other methods of knowing about it. Anyway, he locates it with his waving whiskers, and when he locates it, presto! it's gone.

This fish has never been recorded as over about six inches long, and aquarium specimens are large when they are half that.

From far-away India is another Catfish of the same general appearance, but of more standard coloration. At least, those few specimens under observation always exhibited the same color of silver brown or green, according to the light in which they are viewed, with a few light lines down the body. The lines are really only suggestions of lines, being hardly visible. These fish do the same things in approximately the same manner as *Pimelodella gracilis,* although they are reported to deposit adhesive eggs on plants, but the same specimens, in many moons, have never shown any sexual activity at all.

Once in a while, a few small specimens of *Pimelodus clarias* appear in a shipment of South American fishes. This is another fish known as the South American Catfish, and is a very useful scavenger. It is grayish or brown in color, and reaches a foot or so in length, but not usually in an aquarium where its greatest length is not more than four or five inches if it was shorter than that when it was brought in. While little is known of its life history, we do know that it will live under quite terrible conditions for several years, not seeming to be discommoded in the least by bad water. It does not bother moving fishes at all; so it may be safely included in a tank of peaceful animals as a scavenger.

It might be as well to explain here that many of the Catfishes make startling dashes to the surface of the water from their usual place at the bottom of the tank. This is apparently for the purpose of obtaining a mouthful of air, which they use to a certain extent for they are not exclusively dependent upon the dissolved oxygen in the water. It is this ability to use atmospheric air which enables them to survive the effects of foul water that would kill other fishes.

A very pretty little Naked Catfish is the Harlequin. This, *Pseudopimelodus parahybæ,* is brown, with black wavy lines covering a good proportion of its body. The fins are marked in a similar fashion. Although the length of a full-grown specimen is about six inches, most of the fish imported are not above an inch or two long. They are broad at the front of the body, tapering off to the tail, and remind one somewhat of a rather beautifully marked tadpole. However, this fish is very shy, spending the greater part of its life hidden away in as undisturbed a corner of the aquarium as it can find, although it will wriggle into a mass of vegetation if there is any available. Its sucker mouth is an efficient, but small, vacuum cleaner, for, while it does not eat any of the decorative plants of the tank, it will very thoroughly clean off all the fuzzy algæ which attach themselves to the leaves of the larger plants. This is an important function, for if the algæ take hold in any quantity, they will sometimes smother the major plants.

To aquarists who are a little nervous about the damage some of the larger Catfish might do to a beautifully planted aquarium, this little fellow is a windfall, for in its unobtrusive manner it is an excellent scavenger, cleaning up all sorts of débris, and its more or less permanently small size renders its most excited wriggles ineffectual in the uprooting of plants.

Before we leave this débris-eating group, we must mention the Spiny Catfish, *Doras cataphractus*. This too is classified as a Naked Cat, although anything it lacks in scales is amply made up in spines.

This Doras is a flat fish, dark brown or black in color. Its pectoral fins are armed with hard, hooked spines on both edges as well as small teeth on the outer surface, while along the sides of its body run a series of bony plates, on whose outer surfaces are innumerable sharp spines or various sizes.

Mature specimens are about three inches long and will stand almost any sort of abuse. When they are lifted from the water, they make a small buzzing noise. The fish can shut its fins close up against the body where the spines of fin and body appear to interlock and would seem to form a very efficient vise in which to hold anything. Just what they would hold, however, is problematic, for they are too far away from the mouth to be of any use in catching and holding food, and the fish does not seem to use them to hold on to anything fixed to prevent its being swept away by swiftly flowing water. In the wild state, they may do this; I don't know. I do know that the spines are so scattered over the body and so strongly developed that it is almost impossible to remove the fish from an ordinary net. To save the fish from losing half his armor when he has to be moved, the only practical tool is a net made of silk. He cannot stick to this material at all.

Another fish, often sold especially as a scavenger, is the Weatherfish. It is, however, more of a nuisance than a help, for it is continually digging into the sand at the bottom of the tank and uprooting all the plants.

Specimens sold as Weatherfish have been variously identified as *Misgurnus misgurnus* and *Cobitis fossilis,* two related species with the same burrowing proclivities. The long, slender, round shape of the body enables them to dive into the sand almost as easily as they dive through water, and their habit of lying with just the mouth, with its surrounding whiskers, showing above the level of the sand, makes them look ludicrous. Sometimes these fishes drape themselves gracefully in the leaves of plants, but they dash off with great speed if they are disturbed. When they are investigating the surroundings for something to eat, the six barbels about the mouth wriggle and move about for all the world like the chin whiskers of the backwoods farmer of cartoon fame. They are natives of Europe and Asia, and grow long enough to make the *pièce de résistance* of human meals in their own native lands.

They have been reported as spawning in masses of floating plants, depositing several thousand eggs at a time, but the plants are not always essential, for pairs of these fishes have spawned in tanks where there were no plants of any sort, although the eggs were never observed—only the tiny babies.

The name Weatherfish comes from their supposed ability to detect approaching changes of weather. On such occasions they are supposed to dash about the tank frantically. There is some basis of truth behind this reputation, but just where or what their barometer is no one has discovered. As scavengers, some of the Catfishes are preferable, for they are not as hard on the plants of the tank.

# Appendix

Since this book was prepared there have been some changes in the practices of fish keepers; some additions to the number of fishes available; and some additions to our knowledge of the habits of fishes, the conditions they require to prosper, and the actual happenings inside the tank.

Many of these latter are more apparent than real, as, for instance, a recently reported measure for the control of the disease, Velvet, in which the effective agent is a bit of copper mosquito wire. It is the copper, of course, which controls the disease, the use of mosquito gauze being incidental. More than fifty years ago the European fanciers were using copper pennies for the same purpose. They didn't call the disease Velvet, but it was the same thing they were after, a method of keeping the water in such condition that the fishes kept well and the disease agents were held to a minimum.

Even so, a discussion of some of the methods in use, their causes and effects, an enlargement of some of the things hinted at in the earlier work, and some comments about fishes which have appeared in the last few years, will put much of the information available to the more recent fanciers into a perspective which sometimes seems to be lacking entirely.

What is apparent at once to anyone who has been interested in fishes at all is the tremendous increase in the numbers of people who keep fishes for fun and pleasure and the enormous increase in the size of the industries which service them. What is equally apparent is that fishes don't change much in either behavior or requirements, and basically, fanciers don't change much either. They have different gadgets to play with, both mechanical and chemical; use different names for many of the old standbys; have, relatively, an extremely wide selection of fishes to choose from, offered in what, by the standard of even twenty years ago, are palatial fish parlors. Their problems, passions, selections, however, are fundamentally the same and we receive the same questions and listen to the same discussions, arguments, and aspirations we listened to before many present-day fanciers were born.

It is difficult to decide which is most important as a starting point. It is obvious that fishes can't live without water, so that water might well be used as a starting point, but there is no point in talking about water unless the fishes are available to be kept in it. Likewise, there is no point in talking about either if there is no suitable container to put both into. Fortunately for the fancier, there is a wide stock of all sizes and shapes of tanks to select from. In spite of all efforts to the contrary, most fishes have never learned how to live properly in a tank of the wrong proportions and it is essential that no matter what shape or style of tank may be used, it should always be shallower than its smallest surface dimension. For special purposes, high narrow tanks, such as those fitted into a picture frame affair, will serve, but they are not intended to, nor do they, maintain fishes in good condition indefinitely. Tank manufacturers and dealers have learned this, and although there is a great variety of tanks available, most of them conform to this specification.

The apparent discrepancy in these dimensions in smaller tanks is not an acutal discrepancy, for although a two-gallon tank, for instance, is only 6½ inches wide and 8¼ high on the outside, one will find, when the tank is set up, that there is usually not more than six inches of water in the tank by about six inches of water wide, the differences being taken up by sand at the bottom and air at the top of the water.

There is a fundamental reason behind this. It is that, all discussions otherwise, the fishes live on the oxygen dissolved in the water, using it up and replacing it with carbon dioxide which will suffocate them unless there is a maximum surface area to the body of water, in relation to the cube of it, to permit the proper exchange of these gases. Anyone who doubts this can quickly and disastrously prove it to himself by taking any standard tank in good condition and with a stable population of fishes, and merely floating on the surface some slabs of wood, suitably waterproofed by being coated with paraffin. As the area of the wood increases, the number of fishes dying in the tank also increases, indicating that all other things being unchanged, the lessening of the surface area in respect to the cubic contents of the water is critical.

However, as we say, tanks of other shapes and proportions may be used for special purposes and for a short while without, in most cases, serious loss.

The material of the frame of the tank is often discussed as being of some importance. Actually it isn't very important, as long as it is rigid enough to stand up against the weight of water in the tank, for the frame is, or should be, completely insulated from the water by the glass and slate of the sides and bottom, and by the cement which makes the assembly watertight. There is one point in the frame of the tank which is exposed to the action of the water, however, and which should be protected by one means or another. This is the inside of the top member, the part of the frame which surrounds the top of the glass walls. This is subjected to the action of water which has evaporated from the tank and condensed at that point and thereafter drops down. If the metal in the frame is of improper material, or is not protected, it can eventually load the water with enough dissolved material to cause the fish trouble. It can also deteriorate badly, and ruin the tank. This member, then, should be coated with some protective covering. We have found the best material for this purpose to be black asphaltum varnish, applied in two or three thin coats. Transparent nail polish will serve, or any other fairly inert coating material; but paraffin, for instance, which is otherwise ideal, is too soft and will lift off. Since it is not in sight, the color is of little importance.

Right after World War 2, plastic tanks of one sort or another were offered for sale, and a few may still be found. These are not really very good, unfortunately, for a number of reasons, but the main one is that the plastic is so soft that it scratches easily and spoils.

The water is of course of the utmost importance, for the fishes are virtually a part of it, or rather, it is virtually a part of them. They live in a much more intimate relationship with it than we do with our surrounding air, for instance; and changes, even subtle ones which are not readily identified or even impossible to identify by any laboratory methods, have sometimes the utmost effect on the fishes. As an extreme case, there are some sea-water fishes which cannot stay alive in water taken exactly at the spot where they have been living but which has been kept in glass vessels for as little as twenty-four hours. This is an extreme, but even so, all fishes are somewhat in the same pickle in respect to the water. In actual practice, the ordinary pet fishes are all from fresh water and are all from streams or ponds which are likely to be changed, even considerably changed, by rain storms or spring freshets, or from swampy areas which periodically dry up or almost dry up, subjecting the fishes to all sorts of changes in the chemical structure of the water, of gas pressures, and of contained salts of one kind or another, and to great varieties in temperature. It is only fishes which can withstand the effects of such changes that we can keep in tanks, and even at that, they are quite frequently so close to the edges of their tolerance that a small additional change, such as a change in temperature which they would survive in nature, becomes fatal to them in the tank.

In most civilized communities, however, the ordinary drinking water available is within the limits of safety for the fishes. It is quite possible, and it has been done many times, to establish a tank which will support fishes for as long as twenty years without changing the water, a little being added from time to time to make up for evaporation.

In such tanks the water has gone through a definite cycle which is called "conditioning." Exactly what happens, or why it happens, when water becomes conditioned is almost unknown, but we know part of what happens, and we know the end result. A tank of freshly-drawn water is usually water from a supply originating in a lake or reservoir which has a normal population of one kind or another of fish and all the standard biological factors concomitant with their living. The water is filtered and treated with chemicals, usually chlorine, to remove gross particles and most of any bacteria there may be in it. This makes it potable. When the water is drawn from the faucet, the actual drawing of the water removes a good proportion of the chlorine. Allowing the water to stand exposed to the atmosphere, removes virtually all the remainder.

No matter what else is done, it is advisable to remove any possible chlorine first.

When this has been removed, the water, having been exposed to air for even a few minutes, or exposed more or less continuously, as is more normal in an aquarium, is invaded by airborne bacteria, spores of fungi, all sorts of things, which settle on it, and finding a good culture for growth, start to grow and multiply. The addition of fishes, with their contribution of waste products, enriches this culture medium, and a cycle commences. A good growth of bacteria, mostly *Escherichia coli,* develops, even to the extent of making the water cloudy or milky. Along with this, however, grows some sort of limiting agent, the peak of growth of the latter being a day or so behind the peak of the bacterial growth. Between population pressures, the eating of all the available food by the bacteria, and this limiting factor, the bacteria are destroyed almost completely, and the water reaches an asymptote, which is a not quite constant line of population of bacteria, somewhat less than that which was in the water when it was freshly drawn. If the number of fishes introduced into the tank is not too great, and if the feeding of the fishes during this period is at the minimum, the cycle will last about ten days, the water at the end of this period being very clear, clean, and of such stable biological balance that the introduction of any but the most excessive amounts of food materials cannot throw it off balance. Such water is "conditioned" water, and is what the fancier must have if he is to keep his fishes in any kind of condition at all.

The selective dying of fishes in mixed groups does not always follow mistreatment of the tank. Along with the basic conditioning of the tank water is another kind of conditioning which is done by the fishes themselves to suit themselves. It is an unconscious operation, of course, as far as the fishes are concerned, and it is so delicate and obscure that it can't be analyzed in the laboratory. It can be demonstrated in tanks, however. In such conditioning, each species of fish automatically strives to make the water most suitable to its own species. Many species may make it so much alike that there is no essential difference, as far as the fishes are concerned, but there are other species which seem to be almost antagonistic to each other. In such conditions a tank of such antithetical groups may go along fairly well for some time, none of the fishes being actually sick, but none of them really thriving. This is usually manifested in the lack of breeding of fishes which otherwise seem all right, and is most commonly found in the so-called "community tanks." In such tanks, it is natural for fish to die of old age once every so often. If the balance between the two or more kinds of fishes in the tank is delicate, the groups which have not lost a member immediately are in the ascendancy in this balancing and thus a pressure of unsuitable water for the group which has lost a member is initiated. In tanks of long standing, which originally started with a well-mixed community and which have not been interfered with, it is sometimes noticeable that the predominant population is one kind of fish—all Barbs of one sort or another, or all live-bearers, the others gradually disappearing. In tanks of still longer standing, if the fancier wishes to try, he will find that eventually there will be only one species in the tank. This is not theory, it actually happens. The only theoretical part is why it happens. However, most fanciers interested in keeping fishes have already found that their community tanks need more or less constant adjustment if they are to remain in the original concept of them—a well-matched group of fishes of different sizes, shapes, and colors—while if fishes are to be spawned and bred, it is desirable to put these into tanks by themselves.

All this is part of the conditioning of the fish tank and explains, in a minor degree, the statement that the fishes live in intimate relationship with the surrounding water.

Sea-water tanks are in great demand, and have been for some time, the interest and demand fluctuating somewhat but never being without some devotees whose work, both mental and physical, really deserves a better return.

Actually, no one has really managed to establish a sea-water tank, or even a big system, which is permanent in the way that the tropical fish tank is permanent, the length of time the water remaining good being proportionate to the amount of water in the system.

There are some wonderful small marine fishes which could

be made available for fanciers, fishes which are beautifully colored and which have remarkably interesting habits, but their keeping still depends upon the ability of the fancier to keep a constant supply of good sea-water available to them. In most places this is a problem which is not easily solved, but which may be overcome for a while if a number of glass vessels can be filled with good sea-water which is not polluted or diluted with waters from sewers or streams. There are a few places along the shores where suitable water may be procured, but since a single five gallon jug is heavy, and five gallons isn't very much in a fish tank, the problem of getting sufficient water is not readily mastered. If a number of five gallon bottles can be filled with good water and kept in a cool dark place, one is on the road to keeping a marine tank. A tank of water will last for a month or two before it is spoiled for at least a few of the fishes which could be procured. As the water evaporates, it may be made up with ordinary faucet water, and when it spoils or discolors, as it will sooner or later, it may be replaced, or part of it replaced, with new water from the cache in the bottles.

The operation of a sea-water tank for any kind of fish is kept at its best by moving the water. A still water tank such as the so-called balanced tank never seems to work, but a small pumping system, using airlift pumps, will do for a while. The water is quite active, chemically, however, and metals of all sorts are best kept out of it. In addition, all but a few marine fishes are highly sensitive to temperature changes, not having learned, as many fresh water fishes have, to adjust to fluctuations. It is desirable to have adequate and dependable heating units and thermostats in a sea-water system.

Artificial sea-waters have been compounded in great numbers, but none that we ever heard of or tried have really worked well, although they will do for a short while for the small, hardy, sea creatures one finds along the shores of bays and inlets. They are not usually good enough for fishes from reefs or open water. They are useful, too, in mixing with normal sea-water, so that a given amount of good ocean water will last longer if mixed with these solutions. However, a ten gallon tank of normal ocean water will last longer than one of the same size of mixed water.

The procurement of good sea-water is a problem for many people besides fish fanciers. Obviously the fanciers would like to keep sea-water fishes—for what could be nicer than young Angel Fishes of the several species available about the shores of Florida, or than the Clown Fishes and their relatives of the Far East, and who would not like to keep Sea-horses which are available in great numbers along the eastern seaboard from time to time—but the demand is far greater than this. All large public aquaria need sea-water and must go to great trouble and cost to get it, and there are innumerable laboratories, both biological and medical, whose work is greatly hampered by their inability to procure and hold sufficient good sea-water to maintain some marine fishes of great importance in research. A large proportion of the fishing industry, particularly the lobster fishery, has spent a great deal of time and money working on artificial or even stored sea-water, without good results to date.

Even so, as we said, a few hardy marine creatures can be kept for a while if some sea-water is procured and kept, and eked out sometimes with an admixture of artificial sea-water, kept in motion, as we said, by some non-metallic pumping arrangement. Fortunately, almost every fish, including Sea-horses, which may be kept in such water will eat the same thing, chopped fresh clam, if this is presented to them with some coaxing and patience so that the problem of feeding is somewhat minimal. Time and patience are required, however, and no one should attempt to keep a marine tank without both.

In addition to endeavoring to keep the water, either fresh or salt, in the tank in both chemical and biological balance, it is desirable to keep it tidy and clean, from a housekeeping point of view. No one is particularly proud of a tank which has an accumulation of debris at the bottom of it, even though this may be somewhat natural-looking. For the sake of the fishes, this natural, pond-like accumulation is highly desirable—for most tank fishes, that is—but it is unsightly. Consequently a number of gadgets and devices for the mechanical cleaning of the tank are available and have become popular. These are essentially air pumps, filters, sand stops to keep the sand at the bottom of the tank clean and separate from debris for convenience in siphoning, and a heating element of some sort to keep the water at temperatures suitable to the fishes.

The supply of air to operate the airlift pumps—all ordinary aquarium water pumps are airlift—or to feed distributor or diffuser stones is generated by a small air mover, rather than a compressor type of pump, the air being blown through tubes connecting the pump to the apparatus it must operate. It is seldom under more than an ounce or so of pressure, and the main thing is that if it is started, it should be kept operating without failure. There is a reason other than keeping the tank clean for this, one which we will discuss later. Pumps of all sorts, sizes, and types are available, and for any ordinary tanks, the usual yardstick for their measure is price and the reliability of the vendor.

Types of airlift pumps are also many, but the principle is the same. They operate by mixing air with a column of water contained in a tube open at both ends, the lower end being submerged in the tank and having joined to it the end of the air line, the upper end spilling into a container of some sort, and the subsequent flow of water following a simple principle of gravity by which a heavier body displaces and lifts out of the way a lighter body when the medium is fluid. A column of mixed air and water is lighter than a column of water, so the mixed air and water moves upwards. Such a pump is simplicity itself and while they may be bought already assembled, they may also be made from two pieces of plastic or glass tubing, one finer than the other. The wider one is set into the tank water, the narrower one being turned up and back on itself a short distance. The folded end of the narrow tube is inserted into the bottom of the wider tube. The free end of the narrow tube is connected to the supply of air, the free end of the wider being bent or connected by tubing to the receiving vessel.

The most usual way of hooking this up is to put the pumping apparatus into the part of the filter box which receives the filtered water so that the cleaned water is pumped back into the tank, the filter water level being maintained by a simple strap siphon working between the tank and the primary receiver of the filter. Between this part of the filter and the part into which the cleaned water flows is the filter bed. It is this which actually holds the debris being filtered out. Some people swear by glass wool pads set here; others prefer activated charcoal, or a combination of activated charcoal and glass wool, while still others find ordinary bird gravel or crushed quartz satisfactory.

Water which is being circulated in a tank through a filter by means of these airlift pumps becomes thoroughly aerated, which is to say that all of the water is sooner or later exposed to a water-air interface. This is very important if there is any danger whatever of the tank's being overcrowded, for it increases the effective air-surface-body of water relationship referred to earlier in the discussion of tank shapes. The increased air-water interface helps the release of carbon dioxide, the critical part of any standard aerating system for fishes. Another way of doing this is simply to release the air from the pump into the water in a series of fine bubbles, made by mounting at the end of the air tube a small porous stone or another type of diffuser. These diffusers are available in a number of shapes and styles, all about equally effective.

Sometimes the stones are mounted in the head of a model of a diver or some such ornament set at the bottom of the tank, the air being carried down to the ornament by a rubber tube. If such things seem desirable, and the fancier does not mind changing water more or less frequently, there is no objection to such ornaments, which are made of cast metal, wood, or plastic, but for practical and simplified fish keeping they are best kept out of the tank.

Where there are many tanks, or tanks which are fairly deep, the small pumps previously discussed are not adequate, for as we said, they have little if any pressure. Since a column of water one inch square and twenty-seven inches high, approximately, weighs one pound, it takes slightly more than one pound of air pressure to pump air to the bottom, so that if a tank is deeper than two feet, it is desirable to use a regular air compressor. These are available in a variety of sizes, and are usually used when there is a number of tanks, regardless of their depth.

And while we are at it, and while we are speaking of the air introduced into a tank, it is as well to indicate that a tank which needs such air is one which is not too well able to take care of itself during a power failure. If the air is used simply to keep the water clean, a failure anywhere in the pumping system is not critical, but if the air is used to allow for a greater population of fishes in the tank, the failure of any part of the system may cause many deaths.

It is not usually good practice, except for the cleanliness of the tank to run the pumping system for periods and then turn it off. Gas pressures build up to the detriment of the fishes and, if the number of fishes is critical, some of them are going to die prematurely.

We have mentioned population and overcrowding of the tank several times, but we are unable to define it clearly, or as clearly as some fanciers might like. It is obvious at once that a ten-gallon aquarium will hold one Guppy, and it is probably safe to say that it would hold fifty Guppies, other things being equal, but it is also safe to say that a ten-gallon tank in one location will not hold more than fifty Guppies, while the same tank in another location, will hold one hundred and fifty such fish. The actual population a tank can accommodate varies directly with innumerable factors, some of which may be named; intensity and duration of light, as well as its source and point of origin; temperature; size and condition of the fish themselves; condition of the water; number, size, and kind of plant leaves; and an enormous number of less obvious factors, which include amount and kind of outside disturbance of the tank—including the vibration of the floor or platform upon which the tank rests—in fact, the rule rather than the exception is that no two tanks are ever alike, and no single tank is ever quite the same two days running, so that it becomes impossible to say how many fishes of any kind can live in a tank of any given size or shape. Experienced fanciers have already found they cannot indicate, beyond a certain point, how many fishes any one of their tanks will hold. Most dealers, who are, by and large, reliable in their advice, can give a fair idea of the normal expected population of a given size of tank in average local conditions. Beyond that they cannot be expected to go.

The "balanced aquarium," as it is usually considered, is probably what most people have in mind in establishing any such tank as we have been discussing, in which the water is still, or at most moved through a small filtering system. Actually, there is no such thing as a "balanced" tank. On the face of it, it couldn't be balanced if food has to be put in continually and debris removed, but aside from this somewhat esoteric consideration, the balanced aquarium as it is popularly considered, in which fishes balance plants, and plants fishes, does not exist. Plants have many purposes in the tank, not the least of which is decoration—nothing looks nicer than a well-planted tank— but as a balance for the fishes, and especially as a medium of exchanging or reducing gases developed in the water, they have virtually no value.

Actually, and aside from a faulty concept, it isn't really important as a practical matter, for no one ever could, even if he wanted to, arrive at any continuous equilibrium of the supposed functions of the fishes in relation to the plants or of the plants in relation to the fishes, and so no one really sets up a balanced aquarium even when he thinks he has. They set up a tank of still water, suitably conditioned, introduce suitable fishes, and decorate it as their taste dictates with plants capable of growing under water, and call it a balanced aquarium. Unfortunately, there has been a great deal of misconception about the matter, purely as a concept, but such a mistaken concept has probably not cost anyone any fishes.

Plants per se, however, have a number of values in the tank. They are decorative and they provide cover for fishes which are harassed by others, or are shy, and they are almost essential for the breeding of some kinds of fishes, providing anchorages for eggs or cover for young fry.

The temperature of the water in an aquarium is of extreme importance to most fishes, for having no temperature control within their own bodies, they are dependent upon the temperature of their surrounding water to keep the body processes operating normally. Some few fishes have wide tolerance, particularly those from temperate fresh waters, provided the changes are made gradually, or relatively slowly anyway, but most fishes are unable to adjust rapidly to change and some are hardly able to adjust at all. Since, by definition, most tank fishes are tropical, it follows that somewhat tropical temperatures are needed. These are easily maintained in the tank, even in cool rooms, by aquarium heating units of appropriate size, operated by thermostatic controls. As with all other supplementary apparatus, there are many kinds of heaters available today. For the least interference with the condition of the water, those made of glass are by far the best, and fortunately a number of excellent kinds are available in pyrex glass. Most sturdy are those made in metal, stainless steel, usually, and these are probably the most serviceable in tanks where the water is changed fairly frequently. Metal ones of any kind are unsuitable when it is necessary or desirable to keep the water unchanged for long periods.

While the dealer can help considerably in suggesting a heating unit of proper size for any tank of given size, the amount of radiation of heat from the tank, and consequent cooling of the water, is purely an individual matter, so that if, for instance, a dealer suggests that a sixty-watt heater is normally suitable for a ten-gallon tank in his area, the dealer cannot be held responsible for poor service if the room in which the tank stands is abnormally cool. As a general rule, it might be safer to use a heater one size above what is normally safe, just in case. The extra cost is hardly worth thinking about, but the extra safety factor is enormous.

In lighting the aquarium there have really been changes, for not only have different kinds of lighting fixtures been developed, but even different sources of light. In particular, fluorescent tubes have become available. These are made in a great many colors, and a great many shades, or degrees, of white, and while the fancier normally may not have much use for colored light in his tanks, the degree of white he uses can be of great importance. Standard white light tubes are not very good for the plants—that is, the plants do not usually thrive under them, and daylight white tubes give the tank a moonlight effect. We have found that tubes labelled Warm White, Warm Tint, or the equivalent, neither make the tank weird nor spoil the plants.

In actual practice, however, we have found that since no two tanks ever respond in the same way or to the same degree to almost anything, including either intensity of light or kind of light source, that best results are obtained by being able to mix the light somewhat, adding to, say thirty watts of fluorescent light, one twenty-five watt incandescent bulb. The proportions vary both with the requirements of the tank and with the aesthetics of the keeper. Extremely pleasing effects within the tank may be achieved at small expense and with little time and effort by fiddling with the lights.

This includes, of course, the placing of the light sources. Normally, a tank is viewed from one long side, the front, the plants being arranged at the back and sides, thus keeping the fishes towards the front, with the green acting as a back drop. To observe the color of the fish properly, the light should enter from the top front, which sometimes places it away from the plants. Using two smaller light sources properly placed, the one at the front to light the front sides of the fishes and the other at the back to keep the plants under good stimulation, is a much better system than to use one single light source. Fixtures accommodating both kinds of lights are available and are well worth the expense.

It is taken for granted, of course, that the fancier knows that the best effects from any lighting system follow the use of lights immediately above the tank. Not only do fishes not like side or bottom lighting, but these give poor visual effects for normal purposes, and besides, make for much extra work in removing algae from the glass walls of the tank nearest to the lights.

Feeding of fishes is still the same basic requirement—a reasonable amount of all the food elements necessary to living, best provided by living foods of all sorts. However, while Tubifex is without question the best possible source of living meat for most fishes, being practically all meat rather than a little meat and much shell as are daphnia and insect larva of one sort or another, there are some fair substitutes available. These are canned or boxed mixtures of various food products which many fishes take readily and on which they live fairly well. It should be remembered, however, that there is still no substitute for life, and living food of some sort should be given to all pet fishes at least once in a while. Since virtually all dealers have some living foods available most of the year, it is no real hardship on the part of the keeper to provide a few Tubifex or daphnia for his pets. They will more than repay him in health, growth, color, activity, and possibly spawning.

As a matter of convenience, it is likely that the fancier can only pick up living food once a week or so. For daphnia and such creatures, storage is not usually feasible so that these should be fed off as soon as prepared, making sure that if there has to be any mixture of living and dried food at any single meal, the dried food is fed first. When the appetite of fishes has been somewhat reduced by living food they are not inclined to take the dried food, but when the edge has been taken off with dried food they will still take a fair share of living food afterwards.

Where it is possible to store a small container of living Tubifex in a refrigerator it is just as well to use Tubifex for all feeding, for the normal portion available will feed a number of fishes for a week. The Tubifex does very well if the container is kept closed in the refrigerator at about a temperature of forty degrees or so, normal refrigerator temperature, that is. We have kept some for a month without any difficulty at all. There is no smell, of course, and no possible danger of contamination to any other foods kept in the same box. We have found a standard cardboard container of one quart capacity both suitable for keeping the Tubifex and saving of space. If one has a few more Tubifex than is necessary for a feeding, they may be put into the fish tank where they can live for several weeks if the number is not too excessive, and the fishes will find and eat them as they require.

For very small fishes which are past the infusion stage, Brine Shrimp are probably the best living food. There are many recipes which go into some detail as to the method of arriving at Brine Shrimp, but we have not found over many years' experience, that it is at all necessary to be precise in measuring any of the ingredients. Some water, some salt, and some Brine Shrimp eggs seem all that is necessary. It might be as well to say here that some people seem better able to do things; baking a cake, for instance, simply by using a pinch of this and that and mixing a little, than other people can do following with the utmost precision the most detailed of instructions. In gardening such a gift is known as the green thumb. In fish keeping, or animal keeping of any sort, including the developing of Brine Shrimp, the same kind of thing holds true. Some people can do wonders with no apparent thought or effort while others must struggle a bit. In any case, to about two quarts of water of room temperature add about two teaspoonsful of common salt. When it is dissolved, about an eighth of a teaspoonful of dried Brine Shrimp eggs, available in pet stores, may be added. No mixing is necessary. At ordinary room temperature the eggs will hatch, or a good proportion of them at any rate, in about twenty-four hours. In two days they will be about twice the size they were when hatched, and usually of the right size for feeding two or three day old fry of almost any kind that the fancier finds difficult to feed.

When we are feeding fry with Brine Shrimp we find it desirable to set up at least two such jars a day or so after the parent fish spawn so that even should one jar fail, there will be some Brine Shrimp of suitable size ready for the fry when they need it. Thereafter, we start one jar operating every second day or so for a week, using never more than about four jars altogether; for, as one is exhausted or spoiled, we clean it and start it afresh.

The method of removing the tiny shrimp from the water varies with the individual, there being almost as many ways to do this as there are fanciers. Some people simply take a small dipper of the water and shrimp from the jar and put it into the tank, others siphon off a little directly into the tank, and still others use a fine net of bolting silk or some such finely-woven fabric, pouring a portion of the jar water through it, returning the water to the jar and swishing the shrimp from the wet part of the silk into the fish tank.

From very small fishes, such as the young of Danios, Tetras of one sort or another, and other egg-laying fishes, some fanciers swear by infusions of some kind, and infusion tablets are now available in most fish stores which will, on immersion in suitable water, give rise to more or less heavy populations of one or another kind of almost microscopic living matter. These are more easily prepared than the hay or lettuce infusions of older days. Other fanciers, however, still prefer the crushed yolk of hard boiled eggs as starting food for very young fish. Either seems to work equally well, the question of which is most convenient being, perhaps, the governing factor as to which is used.

In the matter of number of meals per day for small fishes, it is almost obvious that the more small meals a day the better the fishes are. This is something the fancier must work out for himself, as he alone knows the demands on his time. Two or three feedings such as outlined will do very well, but more are very good, if not too much food material is put into the tank at any one time. By extension, this works for adult fishes, too. We have found that the vast majority of fishes thrive on three meals a week, the meals being of such size that the fishes can eat all of the food in ten minutes or so. However, if the fancier can judge the amounts fairly accurately, he can feed three times a day, or even three times an hour. The essential is that there shall be no food left to disintegrate in the tank after any meal.

On the contrary, however, fishes are not always accustomed to regular feeding and most of them can go for quite long stretches of time with nothing obvious to eat. This is of value for people who wish to leave home for a few days. Almost all ordinary kinds of tropical fishes—the kinds normally kept at home—can survive a fast of two weeks without difficulty, provided the tank itself is in good condition. If an absence from home becomes necessary, it is usually a good deal safer to leave the tank completely unattended, securely covered, of course, and shaded a little from any bright sunlight, than to have an inexperienced person try to feed the fishes. Almost invariably, the inexperienced start feeling sorry for the fishes and give them just a touch more food and presto, the tank is in trouble.

For long periods it is best to farm out the fishes to fellow fanciers, or to such of the pet stores which may be able to board them, or else have a fellow fancier who knows one's own particular establishment come in once in a while to take care of the collection. Don't do as a friend of mine once did. He left home for a while, arranging to have a friend stop by at such a time on so and so nights, and then, when he knew the friend would be at his home, called the local police by long distance 'phone and told them a burglar was in his house.

There are still a few fanciers who have the idea that there must be an exact, definite, cut and dried method of caring for any given kind of fish, with exact temperatures, water conditions, depths of water, all included, and that any deviation from this method or set of conditions is wrong. A little reflection would assure them that there is no such exact method of fish keeping, for if such exactness were necessary it would be impossible for us to keep any fishes at all, since it is manifestly impossible for us to duplicate precisely the conditions of some small ditch in the back of yonder up the Amazon, or the Congo, even if we knew what the conditions were.

By a selection which is obvious, only such fishes as can tolerate a fairly wide range of conditions are available for our tanks. Fishes which cannot stand changes never survive capture and transportation. Consequently it is a waste of time to outline specific conditions and methods for the care of any specific species. As a matter of fact, in our own tanks at the New York Aquarium which are normally under the care of one man, times come when that man is away and a second man must take his place. The fundamentals remain the same, but the second man does a number of things, more or less intangible, which are different from those done by the first man, but still the fishes live. There are many fanciers who believe a given method is the only way to do something, while there are just as many who believe a completely different method is the only way, and sometimes both are willing to argue about it at some length and with considerable heat. Actually, both fanciers may be keeping the same kind of fishes with extremely good results, both following the basic fundamentals and varying only in minor points which look widely different and with which the fishes have little or no concern. It becomes, then, silly to set down a set of rules and regulations governing the keeping of this or that species, and equally silly to make a long list of fishes, each with its own set of rules and regulations. Once the fundamentals are mastered—the methods of tank-keeping, of heating, of lighting, of planting, of feeding, and of the mixing of fishes together—the minor details such as the endeavor to establish a specific pH for the spawning of any given kind of fish become quite unimportant, and usually, when stated as facts, are erroneous. As a matter of fact, if the fundamentals are right, these details become of no moment to the fancier either. Many excellent breeders of fishes, both commercial and amateur, of whom we have knowledge, don't know pH from a helicopter, and don't care. They breed fishes well and successfully, and while we have some knowledge of pH, and have a series of laboratories available to us, and have bred fishes of all sorts and conditions from time to time, the one is separate from the other and we do not usually mix them, except, once in a while, to check how wrong a currently popular statement may be. Of course the alkalinity or acidity or salinity of the water can be of great importance in certain circumstances, but they are circumstances not normally found among fanciers at all, most of the arranging of the water, assuming it starts with normal drinking water, being done by the fishes themselves and as part of their actual living. Consequently we do not intend to include a list of recently introduced fishes complete with schedules of their ways of keeping. It would be impossible to do, wrong to try, and quite misleading in any case.

There are some outstanding contributions, however, to the list of specimens available that might be mentioned without loss, not in the order of either their discovery, which is not of great moment for most fanciers, nor necessarily in the phylogenetic order in which they occur, which is likewise of little importance to the fancier.

In any case, a number of different species, new to the fancier, has appeared, most of them fitting nicely into standard community tanks. As may be expected, most of them are Characins, and of these the Neon Tetra, *Hyphessobrycon innesi,* is by far the most outstanding.

This is a small fish, about 1½ inches long, from far up the Amazon, brilliant in blue and red, both sexes being alike externally, for which we must still depend upon importations for most specimens, although a number of spawnings have been reported. Just what we do or do not to suit the fish completely is somewhat of a mystery, for the conditions prevailing in the reported spawning are frequently far apart. Still, a few people have bred them, reporting breeding behavior, even with all the differences of conditions, which might well be a description of the breeding of Tetra von Rio. Apart from the breeding of them, however, it is possible to keep Neons in good shape and condition, as far as appearances go, for several years, either by themselves or with other small fishes.

Some of them have been reported also as carrying some sort of sickness with them. This has seemed to be so specific that is has been called Neon Tetra Disease, but it isn't essential that they have it and we have carried specimens for more than four years without trouble.

No fancier should fail to try a few of these—two enliven the appearance of the tank enormously, and a number in a fairly large tank are marvelous, for they stay in schools, most often when they are new and scared, but at other times too, and as they move their colors are truly one of the sights of life.

The Blind Cave Fish, *Anoptichthys jordani,* a white creature about two inches long without either eyes or eye sockets, from a cave in Mexico, has been established. This strange fish which seemingly has to live on nothing but the droppings of bats in its native cave, and in water which is extremely high in lime content, seems to live without trouble in the lime-free waters of most fanciers' tanks, and on any more or less normal fish diet which it can find without trouble at all, even in competition with eyed fishes.

This fish is very close, taxonomically, to the Mexican Astyanax, and has been crossed with it. In fact, it is possible that the one is merely a form of the other. In any case, the resulting young of the crosses show every kind of development of the eye, from completely eyeless and without sockets, or at least with the sockets covered by scales, to completely eyed forms, and in every possible combination of the two color patterns.

As we said before, these may be kept with other fishes in a

community tank and can successfully compete with them in every way.

This is an indication of the relative unimportance of some of the efforts to match any specific habitat or provide any particular kind of water for one's fishes, for these, from such a highly specialized kind of water, do very well in any normal tropical fish tank.

Cichlids of one sort or another have been brought in, and some which were not, until recently, considered home aquarium fishes, have become more or less popular for small tanks. Probably the best known of the latter group is *Astronotus ocellatus,* potentially as large a fish as any home fancier would want to handle, for it reaches eight or nine inches when full grown, and is correspondingly deep and heavy, as the conventional Cichlid should be. It is an extremely handsome fish which seems to lead a most placid kind of existence, the while swallowing great numbers of any smaller fishes it can find so that it cannot be kept with other fishes unless they are at least as large as itself. Larger specimens are likely to swallow smaller specimens, even blood relations, unless they are separated. Even so, if one has a large tank, up to fifty gallons capacity, these are as interesting and good-looking fish as could be put into it.

While the adults have a very definite pattern of brilliant orange dots, splotches, and a ring which surrounds a jet black spot on either side of the tail, all on an olive background which varies from a greenish gray to almost black, the young develop a great series of markings, changing as they grow, of bars, streaks, and mottlings. At least eight different color patterns have been noticed on young growing in our own tanks, these different patterns apparently being associated quite definitely with the age of the individual.

Although spawning is occasionally accomplished in tanks the species cannot be said to have established themselves as aquarium specimens, most individuals available having been imported as youngsters. We have kept individuals in good color, health, and spawning condition, for fifteen years, so we do not know how long they can live, but once adjusted to a tank they certainly seem to settle down for a good long period.

Like most Cichlids, they are extremely careful about the spawning site, being scrupulously clean and attending to their own strings of eggs and young assiduously, even though they might suddenly decide that there is something wrong with the world and their babies had better be eaten out of it.

Guppies, of course, are still with us, in greater profusion of colors and patterns than ever. This most variable fish, as it would appear, has been offered in a great variety of strains, some of which appear to be reasonably well fixed, although the strains are not always permanently popular and seem to disappear from the general market for a while to reappear sometimes under a new name or under one of the old ones, none of which have any scientific standing but all of which seem to be quite important to fanciers. As a matter of fact, while none of the designs of colors and lengths or styles of fins—the treasured differences which the fancier seeks—have been completely fixed so that every individual born to the selected parents carries the desired characters, some of them do follow the hereditary pattern reasonably well and give great pleasure to whole groups of fanciers.

Strains of the Platy-Swordtail hybrids which are extremely attractive have been established and can be maintained by the careful fancier if he so desires. Not all of these were adventitious, however, but were pleasantly colored side-products of the intensive work of Dr. Myron Gordon of the New York Aquarium in his primary search for the genetical causes of cancer, in which some of the products of such crosses are of immense importance. Side-products or not, however, such fish as the Black Wags are wonderfully attractive for the aquarium. While, as we say, these are products of crossing and recrossing, which might seem somewhat simple to do, we do not think the ordinary fancier is going to have any great success in further developing such things, for the work calls for a great deal of knowledge in the first place and for the kind of care and facilities not usually available to any fancier. Many fanciers seem to think otherwise, however, and we wish them luck in their efforts.

# Index

Habits of feeding, breeding, parental care, courtship, etc., peculiar to individual families or fishes will be found under those groups.